BERLUSCONI'S ITALY

Berlusconi's Italy

Mapping Contemporary Italian Politics

Michael E. Shin and
John A. Agnew

TEMPLE UNIVERSITY PRESS
Philadelphia

TEMPLE UNIVERSITY PRESS
1601 North Broad Street
Philadelphia PA 19122
www.temple.edu/tempress

Text design by Kate Nichols and Matthew Plourde

∞ The paper used in this publication meets the requirements of the American
National Standard for Information Sciences—Permanence of Paper for Printed
Library Materials, ANSI Z39.48-1992

Library of Congress Cataloging-in-Publication Data

Shin, Michael E. (Michael Edward)
  Berlusconi's Italy : mapping contemporary Italian politics / Michael E. Shin
and John A. Agnew.
     p. cm.
  Includes bibliographical references and index.
  ISBN-13: 978-1-59213-716-9 (cloth : alk. paper)
  ISBN-13: 978-1-59213-717-6 (pbk. : alk. paper)
  ISBN-10: 1-59213-716-4 (cloth : alk. paper)
  ISBN-10: 1-59213-717-2 (pbk. : alk. paper)   1. Voting—Italy.   2. Berlusconi,
Silvio, 1936–   3. Elections—Italy—History.   4. Political geography.
5. Italy—Politics and government—1994–   I. Agnew, John A.   II. Title.
  JN5607.S55 2008
  324.945'0929–dc22

2007037132

2 4 6 8 9 7 5 3 1

Table of Contents

Preface

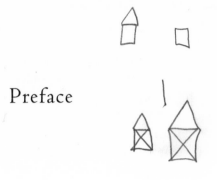

Italy experienced a political watershed in the early 1990s when the old system of parties collapsed and was subsequently replaced. With the new regime emerged several novelties, such as new parties and electoral alliances on both the left and the right of the political spectrum. Perhaps the most notable outcome was the emergence of Italy's wealthiest man, Silvio Berlusconi, as the indispensable focus of Italian politics, both positively and negatively, from 1994 until 2006. Neither Berlusconi's rise to power nor his recent 2006 electoral defeat have met with many detailed empirical analyses of how his and the other organized political forces replaced the old parties. Without neglecting the personal role of *il Cavaliere* (or "the Knight," as he is known and likes to be known), our spotlight falls much more on the geographical dynamics of popular support (or "followership") for the various political factions, particularly on the center-right, to better understand how Berlusconi could assume such a central role in Italian politics.

The conventional story of how Silvio Berlusconi came to power and turned Italy into his fiefdom revolves around his control and use of the main private television networks. We challenge this story as far too simple to account for what actually happened from Berlusconi's initial rise to power in the mid-1990s to his narrow defeat in the 2006 Italian national election. Answering *how* Berlusconi was able to polarize Italian politics around opposing coalitions requires attending to *where* in Italy he initially garnered the most support for himself and his electoral allies. However, in the end, his failure to do so everywhere made him vulnerable to the opposition and its competing constellation of support elsewhere.

Thus, the alternative story told in this book is one that focuses on the geography of Italian politics as essential for understanding what has happened in Italy over the last fifteen years. Moreover, we challenge two more general claims about contemporary electoral politics in Italy and other Western democracies. The first claim, as mentioned above, is that control over the mass media—television, in particular—has essentially removed the influences of geographically grounded social and economic differences from political behavior. The second claim is that geography no longer matters in elections because people have become individualized "opinion" voters without much in the way of any regional differences in how they relate to politics in general or how they vote in national elections. We contend that geography still matters in elections because voters interpret, relate to, and act upon issues differently in different places.

Finally, this book contains a more general message concerning electoral politics in contemporary Europe and North America. Not only are electorates increasingly divided or polarized between left and right—often producing very narrow electoral victories for one side or the other—but there is also an increasing tension for political parties between trying to appeal to the "moderate" or "middle voters," on the one hand, or moving to mobilize voters around more "extremist" agendas (on the right or left) on the other. Berlusconi's attempt to incorporate relatively extreme right-wing parties within his center-right electoral coalition, along with his ability to frame his electoral appeal to a broad "middle" of the national electorate, is an intriguing example of moving in both directions at once.

Several individuals helped us in one way or another to complete this book. In particular, we thank Carlo Brusa, Sebastian Breau,

Carlos Velasquez, Salvatore Vassallo, Piergiorgio Corbetta, Giancarlo Gasperoni, and Simon Parker. We also wish to thank the UCLA Academic Senate Council on Research, the U.S. National Science Foundation and the Cattaneo Institute in Bologna, Italy, for providing research assistance and support related to this book. Finally, we thank our families and friends for their encouragement and support.

I

Introduction: Berlusconi's Italy

I must obey. His art is of such pow'r.
Caliban, referring to Prospero, the unjustly deposed
Duke of Milan.

—WILLIAM SHAKESPEARE, *The Tempest* (act 1, scene 2

*In our country we have never been truly liberated from the need for
a great commander to whom we entrust our lives and free ourselves
from the weight and responsibility of choices.*

—TONINO PERNA, *Destra e Sinistra nell'Europa del XXI
secolo* (Milan: Altreconomia, 2006, p. 11).

July 9, 2006, must have been a day of mixed emotions for Silvio Berlusconi, the former Italian prime minister. The Italian team had won soccer's World Cup with a victory over France, but Berlusconi could not politically bask in the glory of the team to which he had tied his political career. Not only had he named the political party he invented in 1994 to serve his political ambitions after the chant for the national team, Forza Italia, his supporters had also acquired the nickname *gli azzurri* (the blues) after the pet name for the players on the national soccer squad. Since 1994, the story of Italian politics has been dominated by the larger-than-life figure of Berlusconi. When the corruption scandals and investigations of the early 1990s brought down the major parties of government in Italy, Berlusconi made himself a major actor in the emerging new system by organizing a new party and setting about creating a center-right constellation of parties that had never previously existed in Italian politics. He did so partly by mobilizing his own immense resources as Italy's major media baron and by adopting an array of symbols, not the least of which was his involvement in Italian soccer as owner of AC Milan and his connections through that to the national team, to appeal to an Italian electorate disenchanted with old-style politicians and their political parties. However, above all, Berlusconi has provided a political magnet for those Italians less concerned with the normative propriety or probity of national politics, precisely the problem unearthed by the corruption scandals of the early 1990s, and looking to government pragmatically as a solution/barrier to resolving their private problems (see, e.g., Berselli and Cartocci 2006). From this viewpoint, Berlusconi's own career is a metaphor for what some Italians have been looking for in political leadership. What many foreign commentators, most famously the *Economist* magazine, on a number of different occasions over the years, deemed as Berlusconi's "unfitness" to rule Italy, his conflicts of interest in particular, seemed to some voters as indicating a *sagacia* (astuteness) and *fortuna favorevole* (good fortune) that they hoped might rub off on them.

Leadership versus "Followership"

Berlusconi's media ownership and performance as a businessman-politician has come to dominate many accounts, both popular and academic, of Italian politics since the break-up of the old system in 1992 (see, e.g., Novelli 1995; McCarthy 1996; Zolo 1999; Ginsborg 2004a; Andrews 2005; Venturino 2005; Campus 2006a; Stille 2006; Lazar 2007). We refer to many of these accounts more specifically in Chapters 2 and 4. Berlusconi is often seen as the master shaman or trickster of contemporary Italy, manipulating his way to the top through mafia methods (and real Mafia connections) and then by appealing to the crassest and most vulgar aspects of Italian society. We explicitly acknowledge his importance as the organizer and salesman of the Italian center-right by titling this book the way we have. But, in our view, "Berlusconi's Italy" has only been partially of his making. Some of the thrust of this book lies in showing how he has clearly recognized and shrewdly navigated politically around the socioeconomic and ideological cleavages of Italian society. But we give much more attention than is typical to these cleavages and how they operate electorally. Berlusconi may have proved necessary to the past fifteen years of Italian politics, but it is clear that his role alone is insufficient in adequately explaining what has happened.

Italy is famously divided geographically along economic and sociocultural lines. It has long had a "southern question," the problem of the South's lower level of economic development compared to the North (e.g., Valussi 1987; Barbagallo 1994). More recently, with the growth of the Northern League and its campaign against "Roman" rule because of putative fiscal bias in favor of the South, the country has acquired a "northern question." Long-standing regional differences in affiliation with the Catholic Church and in the development of municipal socialism and trade unionism, as well as in collective memory of Fascism and resistance against it have also had profound effects on political sensibilities (Trigilia 1986; Agnew 2002, Chapters 5 and 6). Italy also is famously divided among city-regions that have historically provided a more powerful source for political identities than has the "nation" as a whole. Of course, the spread of a peculiarly "diffuse urbanization" since the 1950s has weakened the cultural grip of the older geographically compact city-regions. Today, much more of the Italian population lives in the diffuse and disordered peripheries of large metropolitan complexes than in the discretely defined *paesi* of historical memory (e.g., Paba and Paloscia 1994). In this context, national electoral success does not come easily. The old electoral system (1953–1992) never produced one party with a nationwide majority of seats in the Chamber of Deputies and the Senate (the two equally powerful national legislative bodies). Governments were always coalitions of parties put together after elections. They rarely lasted long in office and always excluded both the Communist left (PCI) and Fascist right (MSI). All of the parties had clear geographical bases in different parts of the countries, even if by 1976 the PCI and Christian Democrats (DC) had become relatively "nationalized" parties in terms of the geographical spread of their votes. Yet, there was an electoral bipolarism implicit in the old system. When voters switched votes they tended to do so within "families" of parties, moving to ideologically adjacent rather than more ideologically distant parties.

The new electoral system introduced in 1993 placed a premium on the ability of the political parties to group themselves together into alliances so as to facilitate the election of a mix of single-member district representatives (majoritarian) and multimember district representatives (proportional). The idea was to encourage a greater bipolarism in the possibility of governments from opposite ends of a left-right political spectrum or translate the basic bipolarity of postwar Italian electoral politics into the possibility of alliances between clusters of parties that would present a common face as potential governments to the electorate before elections. In this way the blocked alternation between political "sides" and the short-lived governments of the old system would both be consigned to history. This was one of the goals of prescient observers long before the collapse of the old party system in 1992 (for example, see Pasquino 1985). In many respects this is what has happened (even with the return, under Berlusconi's hand, to a significantly proportional electoral system in 2005 as the leader and his allies feared for their political lives) (Berselli and Cartocci 2001; Berselli and Cartocci 2006; Pappalardo 2006). Certainly the 2001 election indicated a significant consolidation of a bipolar polity with "third forces" largely disappearing but with small parties still able to gain a higher degree of representation within the coalitions than their total numbers of votes would mandate (e.g., the Christian Democratic Union (UDC) on the center-right and the Italian Communists on the center-left). Overall, however, the new electoral system seemed to have begun to operate as an instrument of electoral socialization rather than as yet another failed reform simply reflecting the persistence of the political culture of the old regime (Cartocci 2004, but also see Bull and Pasquino 2007).

A downside of increased bipolarity has been an increasingly rancorous style of politics, particularly during election campaigns. Over the years 1994 to 2006, the tendency, initiated by Berlusconi but with avid response from his opponents, has been to portray political adversaries as enemies by using ever more violent and incendiary language. This violent populism borrows both from the style cultivated first in Italian politics by Umberto Bossi of the Northern League—what the DC politician, Mino Martinazzoli, memorably called "the politics of the bar"—and from the polarizing strategies used by U.S. Republican Party operatives such as Lee Atwater and

Karl Rove with their dual focus on identifying "wedge issues" to attract key voting blocs and negative advertising to insult and vilify the "other side." Hectoring and simplifying thus replace debate and complexity.[1] Berlusconi has openly borrowed both advisers and strategies from the right-wing American electoral "playbook." In this regard he is not so much a model that Americans should beware of (pace Stille 2006) as a product of the export of the very system now in place in American electoral politics.[2]

Beyond the changes in electoral system, the period since 1994 has been one of rapid and widespread change in Italian politics and society (Guarnieri 2006; Bull and Newell 2006, Chapter 3). Not only did the major parties of government, the DC and the Italian Socialist Party (PSI), disappear in 1993 in the face of scandal, the PCI had already divided with the collapse of state socialism in the former Soviet Union, and a significant portion of the northern electorate was drifting toward the Northern League and its radically anti-Roman rhetoric. If in the 1980s a political inertia characterized the country, with government policies and public attitudes more like those that had prevailed in Britain and Germany in the 1970s and before—with for example, widespread popular commitment to government price controls, state ownership of major industries, protection of employment levels irrespective of market dynamism, and with limited swings in votes between political parties—all of this began to change in the 1990s. Some have put this down to purely domestic factors, such as the arrival of Berlusconi as a major political actor, whereas others have given more emphasis to the pressures and opportunities arising from the renewed burst of activity in the European Union following the Single Market and Maastricht Agreements that set Italy on course to lowering tariff barriers and joining the euro. Lurking in the background, however, along with the invocation of "Europe" (meaning the EU) as a source of discipline upon a profligate people, has been the perception of an increasingly negative impact of globalization on many of Italy's most important industrial sectors (Ferrera and Gualmini 2004). As a result, the perception of economic danger has become an important element in Italian political discourse both in terms of restricting criticism of government spending restraint and of mobilizing groups afraid for their economic future in an increasingly competitive and unpredictable world economy. If this has led to a sense of an "incomplete transition" from the old system to the new (from the First to the Second Republic) because no policy seems to settle much of anything, it has also reinstated the old fear that Italy is still anomalous in all sorts of ways, primarily in having had its main media mogul as prime minister and in not having two real parties (bipartyism), as opposed to two coalitions of parties that simply parallel its longer-term bipolarity.[3] Why can't Italy be just like an idealized Britain or the United States? Well, as we shall see, at least with respect to electoral politics, although there are all sorts of differences that mandate against Anglo-Saxon bipartyism there are also some important similarities (e.g., the way election campaigns are now run, the use of public power for private purpose, the decline of purely ideological and the rise of personalized politics, etc.) that suggest that Italy is not as anomalous as often alleged (see Sabetti 2000).

The Geographical Dynamics of Italian Politics

The political economy of Italy at the turn of the millennium is not the theme of this book. The geographical basis to Italian electoral politics in the Berlusconi years is our basic theme. By "geographical basis" we do not mean that people in certain places all vote a certain way because they have always done so and because they are all culturally or economically the same. There is a venerable Italian academic tradition—at least there was before the arrival of Berlusconi on the national political scene—of examining Italian electoral politics in terms of distinctive regions with long-standing political "sub-cultures." In our view, when projected from the 1960s into the 1990s this approach confuses what have turned out to be temporary regionally clustered place configurations with a permanent electoral geography. Assuming that new place configurations must necessarily be regional in ways that some of the old ones were, particularly the so-called white and red zones in, respectively, northeastern and central Italy, or that there is "no geography" at all seem equally wrong headed (see Chapter 2).

There is a geographical dynamism to electoral politics. Parties pick up votes in some places and lose them elsewhere, with considerable variance in "swing" from place to place. Places change their relative political complexion with respect to who votes for whom and why. Different types of people (social classes, church members, etc.) in different places also vote differently. Rarely, if ever, is there total unanimity anywhere. But these differences among people in how they vote and how they change their votes in the aggregate over time are always refracted through the "lens" of the significant others (or reference groups) and social processes of learning and everyday experience that are geographically stretched and distributed differentially across Italy.[4]

By way of two examples, after World War II, the city of Lucca in central Italy became a stronghold of the Christian Democratic Party (DC) in a region that was at the same time overwhelmingly drifting to the left. Over the past fifteen years, however, Lucca has become more like neighboring places, as it has also moved toward the center-left (Agnew 2002, Chapter 6). The city of Varese, in Milan's northern hinterland, has seen a much more dramatic movement among locally dominant political forces, from a strong socialist and DC presence immediately after the war, to a place dominated for a while by the Northern League and now where Forza Italia and the Northern League share the largest part of the local electorate (compare Goio et al. 1983 with Agnew 2002, Chapter 7). Other tales of fairly dramatic electoral change rooted in particular places on a par with these can be told from elsewhere in Italy.

A common view, however, is that Italy is becoming electorally homogeneous with the arrival of Berlusconi and his "videocracy." Italy is losing its internal electoral geography. The mass media are usually implicated as the main cause. From this viewpoint, it is Berlusconi's media ownership, in particular, not his salesmanship or organizational skills, which largely explains his success. *Period*. We challenge this view. Even though media of communication, above all television and the Internet, have narrowed the national space by sending out common messages that are received by increasing numbers of the population everywhere, whether people watch the same things or react the same way everywhere is open to serious question.[5] Established everyday routines and conversation settings still mediate between message and reception. This social logic to politics challenges the idea of the isolated rational voter engaging in a calculus of voting disconnected from the rest of life. Though dominant in voting studies, this approach has recently been subjected to important theoretical and empirical critique (see Chapter 2). Moreover, beyond the social influences on voting, cumulative if differentiated across space as they are, people are faced with different "problems" depending on where they live. For example, youth unemployment is much more serious in Naples than in Como, the problem of bad roads is more urgent politically in the industrial Northeast and the hinterland of Milan than it is in rural Calabria, and increasing penalties for tax evasion will disproportionately affect those places where businesses have tighter profit margins and depend more on "off the books" or black labor. Policies that require effective regional administration, particularly those emanating from the European Union involving funds for economic development, likewise create or fail to create distinctive local constituencies depending on the capacity of the regional governments to implement the policies. Such capacities, concentrated in relatively few administrative regions (Tuscany, Emilia-Romagna, Lombardy and Veneto), can become issues in electoral politics: why are "we" failing to capture "our" share of available funds and develop networks with regions elsewhere in the EU? (Fargion et al. 2006). There are also longstanding differences across Italy in how the act of voting is thought of, with a relative concentration of clientelist or patronage voters in the South and more so-called identity /ideological and opinion voters elsewhere (Cartocci 1990). Party organization varies from place to place, and some parties can claim more local "notables" (who can potentially sway the votes of their co-locals) as their representatives than other parties, and often appeal to both local "issues" and to the sensibilities of certain groups whose concerns are shared by the likeminded elsewhere. In other words, people acquire the reasons for how they choose to vote, and the menu of electoral choices available to them is provided through geographically mediated processes.

Berlusconi's political ability and capacity must be judged in this context. We do so by showing how his coalition (along with his party Forza Italia) and the new alliances on the center-left replaced the parties of the old regime through comparing the elections of 1987 and 1992 geographically with those that came after. We distinguish a number of ways in which the old parties were replaced and the new ones became grounded in the ensuing years: switching or substituting, splitting, or colonizing old voters and mobilizing new ones. These geographical processes are the subject of much of the empirical analysis of Italian national election results in Chapters 3 to 5. The specific nature of the processes we identify is discussed at some length in Chapter 3 before we embark on empirical analysis. We use recently developed methods of spatial analysis as the core of our approach in explaining party replacement and affiliation in contemporary Italy. In so many words, we are thus helping "to socialize the pixel [so to speak] by providing a geographic context for social behavior," one of the most exciting frontiers in social science, because "These new [geographic information] tools provide the ability to analyze social behavior across time and geographic scales, although their adoption by social scientists is yet to approach their potential" (Butz and Torrey 2006, 1899). The basic tenet of the approach is that not only electoral affiliations but also changes in such affiliations are best understood in a geographical context.

This is not to say that geographical or ecological methods are totally new to electoral analysis. Over the past thirty years much effort has been put into portraying elections geographically by means of various multivariate ecological models (see, e.g., Dogan and Rokkan 1969; King 2002) and models of information flow and partisanship (see, e.g., Huckfeldt and Sprague 1987; Books and Prysby 1991; Eagles 1995). Yet most of these works ignore rather than take advantage of the fundamental characteristic of geographic data that proximate observations tend to be correlated with each other, and that descriptively this can tell us a tremendous amount about how aggregate votes are correlated geographically and shift over time. In this book we are concerned primarily with describing *how* votes shift or persist geographically in the aggregate across elections and not with making statistical inferences about *why* they do. We do pursue some ideas about why changes occur but these remain speculative if only because of the difficulty of ever definitively transcending the instability of coefficients across different theoretical models (compare, e.g., Putnam 1993 and Solt 2004).

Why, then, if we find this geographical logic so compelling, is so much written about Berlusconi as an electoral magician as if he were all one needed to know about Italian politics? One reason of course is the fact that as well as a leading politician and party leader, he also owns Italy's three private television channels. This basic conflict of interest obviously has given Berlusconi a real advantage over his adversaries in reaching his potential electoral audience. He has also succeeded in personalizing Italian politics, in an American style, when the historic model (at least after Mussolini, and because of him) has been to have parties as the main instruments for electoral competition (e.g., Campus 2006a). However, many commentators are not willing to go beyond this, seeing his electorate as rather like pigeons undergoing operant conditioning. He feeds them; they peck at the right lever. His voters are simply bedazzled or beguiled by him. The power of celebrity is enough in itself to explain his success.

This view of voters is a highly selective one. It presumes that other voters, on the left perhaps, exhibit a greater rationality. Of course, this is an example of the intellectual trap of "false consciousness" that we use when we cannot figure out why people could have done something which we find appalling. The famous quotation, apocryphal or not, of the renowned *New Yorker* magazine film critic, Pauline Kael, is emblematic. When told of Richard Nixon's forty-nine-state landslide in the 1972 U.S. presidential election she reportedly said: "How can that be? I don't know a single person who voted for Nixon." Berlusconi is often regarded today as Nixon was by many commentators in his day. Seemingly, people who would never vote for him are incapable of understanding why others might. In our view, to understand the success of a "toxic" leader such as Berlusconi, to use Lipman-Blumen's (2006) colorful term for leaders who have widespread appeal but whose success undermines institutions and increases collective anxiety, we need to focus on "followership" more than on leadership. Who is drawn to Berlusconi and his coalition and for what reasons?

Political Instrumentalism

Now, if we were Italian voters, we would probably never have voted for Berlusconi. But this is beside the point. Other people did. Berlusconi undoubtedly appeals to some people generally disinterested in politics and looking for a strong-sounding leader. George W. Bush has had much the same appeal. Some of this tendency among Italians is not new at all; even since the demise of Mussolini. Right after World War II a political movement based on *qualunquismo* (meaning literally "man-in-the-street" movement) or noncommitment to existing political divisions had some popular support, particularly in parts of southern Italy. But Berlusconi also is attractive to the legions of people who watch the diet of soap operas, films, and game shows on his television channels. Many of these programs present a particularly vulgar American consumerism as a model way of life. He promises its possibility to them. In this regard, he is like those generations of American politicians who have competed by promising "more." Not surprisingly, those who report watching more of this television are more likely to vote for Forza Italia. But this happens only if the television messages are reinforced and not countered through various social influences that either undermine traditional mores (and produce a more anomic everyday social environment) or work to discount or reduce the allure of the messages. Television, therefore, cannot be expected to have exactly the same effects everywhere.

Berlusconi's seemingly anachronistic "anti-Communism," a favorite theme of his election campaigns, needs understanding in this context. It draws attention to both the collapse of the actual state socialism with which some of his political enemies were once closely associated and the view of the state which he represents. If you vote for them, he is saying, you are voting not only for the failure of central planning (as in the former Soviet Union and Eastern Europe) but also, and more crucially, for what Adam Przeworski (1991, 7) has termed "the project of basing society on disinterested cooperation—the possibility of dissociating social contribution from individual rewards." Berlusconi thus represents something increasingly common across the Western democracies since the 1970s: the idea that, as Ronald Reagan said, government is not the solution, it is the problem. From this perspective, there is no such thing as a public interest beyond the aggregated preferences of individual persons. Margaret Thatcher, another of Berlusconi's heroes, once said: "There is no such thing as society." This logic will draw support from those who worry about the fiscal consequences of too much government spending because of "free riding" by those who do not have to pay the bills. But it also feeds neatly into Italy's legion of self-employed businessmen and group self-regulated interests (taxi drivers, pharmacists, etc.) who want to be left alone by government except when it is to their immediate material advantage.[6] In Italy, these types of people are in much greater numbers, in relative terms, than in most other European countries—and particularly dense in all of Italy's major cities and in the industrial districts of northern Italy. They see themselves as "innocents" in a system that encourages an instrumental approach to law (Diamanti 2006a). That this is hardly totally unique to Italy is worth reiterating, particularly in light of recent corruption scandals and payoffs to political paymasters in the United States and Britain (Sabetti 2000; Sciolla 2004).

The potential Forza Italia voter knows exactly what Berlusconi means when he invokes anti-Communism. This is not at all the same thing as the anti-Communism of the old Christian Democratic Party. That was about affiliations with the Catholic Church and NATO. This is all about *me*. Talk about rationality. From this point of view, rules and laws are not absolute or normative but respected only insofar as they make sense to you in the context of your life (Bailey 2001).[7] Berlusconi is the role model sine qua non for this pragmatic or instrumental approach to politics, but it is one that predated his appearance on the Italian political scene.[8] Clearly, however, after many years of seeing center-right governments at work in the United States, Italy, and elsewhere, none of this necessarily means the actual shrinkage of government. Indeed, as argued in Chapter 4, and notwithstanding much neoliberal rhetoric, Berlusconi and his allies became as proficient at "big-government conservatism" during their years in office as their U.S. counterpart, the George W. Bush administration. Partly this is because other constituencies with greater demands on government—pensioners, government employees, etc.—had also to be attracted into the fold. In Italy many of these people live in different relative densities in different places from those looking for government to be kept out of their pockets (Chapter 4). Thus, there is a geography to both patronage politics and tax revolt. Berlusconi has had to cater to both to win national elections.

Italian society, then, hardly appears here in the same light as it does when the focus is on devious political magicians seducing the populace or on an innocent civil society undermined by devilish political institutions (such as political parties). Such views, both academic and popular, complement that of the media obsession (e.g., Rodriguez 1994; Livolsi and Volli 1995; Sbisà 1996; Zolo 1999; Ginsborg 2004b; Andrews 2005). In 2006, and not very differently from the 2001 election (if with a different electoral system), the Italian electorate split more or less down the middle in its support for the two main political coalitions. Berlusconi, and his allies, then, do have mass appeal. It is a peculiar intellectual blindness to regard this electorate as consisting entirely of political dopes. Civil society is not always "civil" in the ways we might like; it can be remarkably uncivil even when based apparently on such "good" things as solidarity and association (Cazzola 1992; Sapelli 1997; Chambers and Kopstein 2001). The attitude toward Berlusconi voters is akin to the dismissal of poor, religious-oriented voters in the United States who vote for far-right candidates as not knowing their own interests, as if they were not entirely clear about where they stand (e.g., Frank 2005). Now, how they reach the positions they do is something else again. This can be studied and even, perhaps, understood.

Book Overview

As we shall see, there are some important continuities between past and present in Italy's electoral geography. Although Forza Italia's voters are hardly carbon copies of old DC ones, and DC voters have split up in complex ways, at an oversimplified level, the following generalizations make some sense: if the North and Sicily have become the heartland of the center-right over the period 1994–2006, central Italy has remained largely in the hands of the center-left if much weaker now than previously, as it had been since the 1950s, with the peninsula South emerging as the zone where elections seem increasingly to be decided in terms of the national distribution of seats in the Italian Parliament. Although, of course, given the closeness of the 2006 election, it was the newly given vote of Italians resident abroad that actually determined the final outcome in terms of seats. However, the regional labels are potentially misleading, if only because over the past twenty years place configurations in relation to national elections have become less compact or regionalized geographically.

This is an important theme of Chapter 2, which provides an overview of Italian electoral geography between 1994 and 2006 with respect to the potential movement from bipolarism to bipolarity (as we have defined them), a discussion of the 1993 electoral system and the major changes of 2005, and a general review of economic and social trends producing more localized electorates all over Italy but particularly in the North and South. The subsequent three chapters take up the story of the collapse of the old party system between 1987 and 1994 (Chapter 3), the emergence of Berlusconi as a major actor and his impact on the new system along with those of his allies and his adversaries between 1994 and 2001 (Chapter 4), and the ways Berlusconi prepared for but ultimately lost out in the 2006 election (Chapter 5). In the Conclusion we review the overall evidence for a geographical logic to Italian electoral politics during the Berlusconi years and speculate on Berlusconi's future role (if any) in light of his recent behavior and what the results of the 2006 constitutional referendum may tell us about emerging possibilities for the Italian center-right after Berlusconi.

2

The Geography of the New
Bipolarity, 1994–2006

One of the high hopes of the early 1990s was that following the cleansing of the corruption associated with the party regime of the cold war period, Italy could become a "normal country." There were hopes that bipolar politics of electoral competition between clearly defined coalitions formed before elections, rather than perpetual domination by the center, would lead to the potential alternating of progressive and conservative forces in national political office and check the systematic corruption of *partitocrazia* based on the jockeying for government offices (and associated powers) after elections (Gundle and Parker 1996). From one viewpoint this has happened. A fragile electoral *bipolarity* between competing center-left and center-right coalitions has seemingly replaced the old system at the national level. Unfortunately, confusion over what is understood by bipolarity has affected judgment by political commentators as to what has been achieved (Franchi 2006). In particular, a populist-plebiscitary conception of elections between rigid blocs who then demonize one another and fail to recognize any deliberative function for parliament once in office has been confused with the need for bipolar competition at election time (Sartori 2006a; Berselli and Cartocci 2006).

But in another respect, a persistent feature of Italian electoral politics is the continuing lack of electoral bipolarity at other geographical scales, such as the regional and local. Politically, Italy remains a "geographical expression" with little evidence of either emerging nationwide swing between party groupings or of that opinion voting in which any voter anywhere is potentially available to vote for any party. There is also an absence of institutional *bipolarism* in the sense of true left and right parties replacing the ad hoc arrangements at work in what remain strange and often ideologically incoherent coalitions. Indeed, from this viewpoint, the old system organized around the two "spheres" of DC and the PCI was more truly bipolar but obviously had an inability to produce alternation in office between the two sides (Bogaards 2005).

However, the whole concept of a "normal country" this discussion circulates around is deeply problematic. It is based on an idealized model of electoral politics in Britain and the United States, which countries presumably lack the geographical and ideological fractures of Italy and, as a result, effortlessly produce alternation in national office between distinctive left- and right-leaning political forces (Agnew 2002, Chapter 4). Of course, Italian politics has many unique features. But geographical variance in support for political parties is not one of them. This is a widespread characteristic of electoral politics around the world. The study of Italian politics, as well as the study of other political systems, has lacked an understanding of why this is the case. Crucial has been the seeming difficulty of thinking geographically about national politics. A certain "methodological nationalism" has immunized scholars against thinking in terms of fractured or variegated national territories. A normative commitment to national unification has further undermined attending to the ways in which political identities and interests are made out of local and regional conditions as well as national-level ones. Michel Foucault (1980, 149) has captured most vividly what seems to have happened in conventional thinking about space and time:

Space was treated as the dead, the fixed, the undialectical, the immobile. Time, on the contrary, was richness, fecundity, life, dialectic. . . . The use of spatial terms seems to have the air of an anti-history. If one started to talk in terms of space that meant that one was hostile to time. It meant, as the fools say, that one "denied history. . . ." They didn't understand that space . . . meant the throwing into relief of processes— historical ones, needless to say—of power.

As Foucault was suggesting, the devaluation of spatial thinking is a well-established intellectual tradition in its own right. So, it is no surprise that thinking about Italian politics should follow a similar logic—except, that is, because there can be few countries that would seem to be so ripe for the application of spatial thinking. Not only is Italy obviously divided geographically by significant economic and cultural cleavages, its politics has often been understood in spatial terms by students of the "southern question"—the North-South gap in economic development—and of fixed regional political cultures (the red and white zones) as well as by those suggesting more complex typologies of region-based voting processes (exchange or patronage votes in the South, identity votes in the colored zones, and opinion voting in the Northwest) and center-periphery relationships in relative power between central and local governments (Agnew 2002, Chapter 2). Much of this can be traced to the nature of Italian political unification "from above" and the historic difficulty of "nationalizing the masses" around a common set of social identities and interests associated with the national as opposed to other "scales" of social life (Salvadori 1994). As a result, patronage and vote-trading in the interest of geographical constituencies have tended to substitute for less obviously instrumental and more ideological types of mass national politics.[1]

Yet, time and again, influential commentators have announced the immanent demise of a geographically divisible Italy as votes nationalized around two major parties (as in the 1970s with DC and the PCI) or as the media controlled by one man, Silvio Berlusconi, have finally unified the country politically in a nationwide electoral marketplace that is transcending older and now largely residual local and regional mediations (as in recent years). This is the saga reiterated in several of the most popular English accounts of Italian politics since 1992, whatever their own particular virtues in explaining aspects of what has happened (e.g., Andrews 2005; Stille 2006). In this chapter, our primary goal is to challenge the theoretical and empirical adequacy of the vision of a single Italy as the emergent trend of post-1992 Italian electoral politics; albeit because of Berlusconi or more mysterious forces.

In so doing we want to question two more deep-seated theoretical biases in academic political studies that extend well beyond the Italian case. The first of these is the idea of a new politics totally dominated by control over mass media, particularly television, rather than a politics still driven by social affiliations and political-economic divisions mediated by the routines of everyday life. From the two-step flow model of political influence formulated by Katz and Lazarsfeld (1955) to recent studies of the roles of friendship and familial networks and local-environmental effects in the social construction of political outlooks (e.g., Zuckerman 2005), it is clear that media messages are both selected and interpreted according to political orientations that are embedded in networks of social influence. Furthermore, local economic and social issues frequently provide the dominant lens through which national (and other extra-local) messages, claims, and promises are refracted by social networks and thence into political attitudes and voting behavior (see, e.g., Agnew 2002; Golden 2004).

The second theoretical bias is the idea inherited from such intellectual luminaries as Hegel and Durkheim: that modernity is essentially national and that the nation-state provides the singular nexus for modern politics. In other words:

> that national history secures for the contested and contingent nation the false unity of a self-same, national subject evolving through time. This reified history derives from the linear, teleological model of Enlightenment History—which I designate with a capital H to distinguish it from other

modes of figuring the past. It allows the nation-state to see itself as a unique form of community which finds its place in the oppositions between tradition and modernity, hierarchy and equality, empire and nation (Duara 1995: 4).

To Sergio Romano (1993), for example, looking back favorably on the efforts at Italian political unification in the mid–nineteenth century, although alert to the ultimate failure of the later Fascism to fulfill its proclaimed goals, Italy was fatally undermined as an individual subject by the party system of the postwar period. Writing in the immediate aftermath of the *mani pulite* scandals, Romano hoped that "escape" was still possible but only if the veto power of numerous groups within Italian society was neutralized by institutions that departed from the traditions of *trasformismo* (vote trading) and through the encouragement of national-level bipolarity (and alternation) between political forces. Whatever the merits of the details of his discussion, the entire approach rests on the model of nationalist teleology as critiqued by Duara.

We take issue with these biases not by invoking either timeless regional subcultures with different densities of "social capital," the sort of idea made popular for Italy in recent years by Robert Putnam (1993), or other fixed spaces of one sort or another, defined by criteria such as family types, landholding patterns or soils (as in classical electoral geography) (e.g., Solt 2004), but by claiming that dynamic place configurations are central to how the "new" Italian politics is being constructed. By dynamic place configurations we mean the mix of local and extra-local social and economic influences that come together differentially in different places and that change in their conditional effects as the influences themselves are shuffled and displaced over time.[2] These configurations are apparent most obviously in the emerging electoral geography of Italy from 1994 to the present; for example, the South became a zone of competition between the main party coalitions and what Diamanti (2003a) calls a "zona azzurra" of heavy levels of support for Berlusconi's Forza Italia that emerged in the Northwest and Sicily. These patterns, in turn, reflect trends in support for party positions on governmental centralization and devolution, geographical patterns of local economic development, and the reemergence of the North-South divide as a focus for ideological and policy differences between parties and social groups. As Italy is being remade politically, therefore, it remains both one and divisible. Our central thesis (pace Diamanti 2003a, 2003b; and Caramani 2004) is that the historical pendulum does not swing *from* local *to* national (or vice versa), therefore, but constantly *around* these and other geographical scales (through the linkages that both tie places together as well as separate them in their particularity) that although the balance of importance between them changes, there is never a final victory for one, be it either regional or national.[3] Geographical *catenaccio* or lock-down (a term used to describe the defensive style of play in Italian soccer) is not a feature of Italian politics however much it might be desired for ideological or intellectual reasons. Before considering some of the details of post-1992 Italian electoral geography, we want to describe briefly the current conventional wisdom about a nationalizing Italy and to say a little about what we mean by "place and electoral politics."

Envisioning a Single Italy

There are two different versions of the "nationalization thesis" as applied to contemporary Italian electoral politics: if one emphasizes Berlusconi's putative revolutionary use of mass communication to reduce Italy to a single homogenized "public opinion," the other argues for the "return of the state," following a short interregnum in which the "local" and the "periphery" had challenged the authority of the center, and the corresponding homogenization of political opinion around a nationwide menu. The rise of Berlusconi's Forza Italia party, undoubtedly the centerpiece of the center-right alliance since 1994, is seen as particularly representative of this new national homogenization. In both cases, therefore, national politics is seen as operating increasingly without mediation by places or territory. From these perspectives, the question of "where?" is ever more irrelevant to understanding the workings of Italian electoral politics.

The advent of Italian media baron Silvio Berlusconi to national political office as leader of his own political party, Forza Italia (who has twice been prime minister of center-right Liberty Pole/House of Freedoms governments) is frequently interpreted as representing the success of a national "telecratic" model of politics over the old party-based model. In this interpretation, as recounted, for example, by Daniele Zolo (1999), parties no longer call themselves "parties" as such (they are slogans, as in Forza Italia, or known as a Lega (league), Alleanza (alliance), Polo (pole), Casa (house), Rete (network), or Ulivo (olive tree)) and they relate to the public and their voters "in ways that are radically different from those in the past" (Zolo 1999,727). Notoriously, political communication is now largely in the hands of one man through his control over most private and public television channels. More importantly, Berlusconi, has changed the rules of the political game. Other politicians have followed where he led. "Italy has evolved, in less than twenty years," Zolo (1999,728) asserts, "from a neoclassical democratic model, founded on the competitiveness of the multi-party system, to a postclassical democratic model, that is to say, beyond representation, dependent on the television opinion polls and the soundings of public opinion." Reaching all across Italy, television has replaced grassroots organization as the main instrument of political involvement. Thus, "the new politicians no longer belonged to 'parties': they became elites of electoral entrepreneurs who, competing among themselves through advertising, spoke directly to the mass of citizen consumers offering them their symbolic 'products' through the television medium according to precise marketing strategies" (Zolo 1999, 735). As a result, "Not only is political communication almost totally absorbed by television, but so is the whole process of the legitimization of politicians, of the production of consensus and of the definition and negotiation of the issues *that have no other location and, so to speak, no other symbolic places* except television studies and popular entertainment programmes—to which the stars of the political firmament are often invited" (Zolo 1999, 739) (our emphasis).

Television in general and Berlusconi's ability to use it to his advantage have undoubtedly had major effects on Italian electoral politics. Parties do increasingly rely on advertising and polling to push their agendas. Television viewership is relatively higher per capita in Italy (and elsewhere in southern Europe) than in the United States and northern Europe (Wise 2005). Certainly in Italy and elsewhere, celebrity politicians— think of the actor Arnold Schwarzenegger in California, the wrestler Jesse Ventura in Minnesota, the businessman Thaksin Shinawatra in Thailand—have challenged the centrality of professional or machine politicians (Street 2004; Hilder 2005). The personalities of candidates increasingly eclipse the character of parties as major elements in political campaigns (Venturino 2005). Political parties everywhere have also lost much of their capacity to make voters identify strongly with them, perhaps because governments around the world have lost their ability to fulfill what they promise at election time. Specifically, with economies less nationally structured under conditions of globalization, governments are less capable of executing independent economic policies.

But whether these trends, particularly that of the centralization of media control, have had the totalizing effects on national politics alleged by Zolo and others (e.g., Schlesinger 1990, Sbisà 1996; Pagnoncelli 2001; Ginsborg 2004a; Bendicenti 2006) is open to question. For one thing, many segments of the population do not rely as heavily on television for entertainment or information as often alleged. Young people in Italy, for example, are increasingly drawn to radio rather than to television. This is one reason why Berlusconi has recently set his sights on increasing his share of the notoriously fragmented Italian radio business (Taddia 2004). People also tend to watch the television channels and programs that already appeal to them and avoid those that do not. In this regard, television (as with partisan newspapers) tends to reinforce and mobilize already held opinions rather than convert people to new ones.[4] More importantly, opinions are also still formed in everyday interaction with other people, notwithstanding their joint reliance on increasingly homogenized national sources. People in different social groups operating in different milieus interpret what they encounter in viewing television in radically different ways. However persuasive television often appears, the best attempts at persuasion often backfire when people bring their own "common sense" and identities to bear in interpreting what they see (Hall 1980). People are neither as gullible nor as ignorant as either pollsters or media critics often make them appear. (When they are gullible or ignorant, they do not require television to encourage or validate them!) As Giovanni Sartori (1989) has argued, television can also encourage localism more than nationalization. It takes attention off parties and puts it on politicians and their service to constituencies. Thus, television moves simultaneously between the extremes of "no place" and "my place." Any sort of national "good," as inherited from the nationalism of the French Revolution, is lost in between (Sartori 1989, 189).

Finally, Forza Italia's success probably owes more to Berlusconi the politician than in his role as the media baron (see Chapter 4). Not only has he been effective as a coalition builder, at the very least politically mobilizing local business elites and Rotarians all over Italy and bringing together various political forces from the political right, but Forza Italia has become much more of a membership organization than a simple electoral vehicle operated from the offices of Berlusconi's main business, Mediaset (formerly Fininvest).[5] Even Forza Italia has had to organize itself territorially. It seems to have done so relatively successfully in a context in which all parties have lost the kind of local organizational presence some of them (or their progenitors) once had (Poli 2001; Mannheimer 2002). At least in national elections, if not so much in local ones, Forza Italia has been able to supplement its national-level media dominance with local campaign events (in the American style) very much to its benefit.[6] Vital to this success has been the image Berlusconi has cultivated of himself as a persecuted outsider crusading for the interests of other "self-made" people, drawing from the U.S. Republican Party strategy of portraying its electoral adversaries as the "enemies" of ordinary people, which at one and the same time both obfuscates and subtly suggests his own dependence on "persecuted" political connections for his own business and political success.[7] In his very disavowal of insider status his initial dependence on a political mentor, Bettino Craxi, for his business success and his constant run-ins with the judicial system for shady business practices proclaim him as the living symbol of the well-established Italian politics of *raccomandazione* and crony capitalism (see, e.g., Zinn 2001) At the same time, and hardly unique to Italy, Berlusconi also represents the appeal of a person who has made it in business (and as President of AC Milan, in soccer, the most popular sport in the country) who constantly draws attention to the fact that his political adversaries "have never worked." This appeals to those dismayed and alienated from professional politicians and "politics as usual."[8] Even without Berlusconi, therefore, there will be a continuing basis for this aspect of *Berlusconismo* and the emphasis on a populist rapport between the leader and the population at large (Chapter 6). Opportunistic in pursuing themes that appeal to a center-right electorate (such as Catholic objections to fertility treatments, etc.), Berlusconi has worked most actively to blur the distinction between state and market beloved of true liberals, partly to preserve his own vast business interests from competitive pressures (Pasquino 2005; Alesima and Giavazzi 2007).

Paul Ginsborg (2003), hardly insensitive to the role of Berlusconi's media ownership in recent Italian politics (see, e.g., Ginsborg 2004a), argues that too much emphasis on television risks ignoring "the degree to which other forces were at work in Italian modernity, forces which ran counter to any idea of the facile manipulation of the individual." Indeed, the old pre-1992 Italy was dominated by two "churches": the Catholic Church and the Italian Communist Party. Since their relative erosion as political agents, a plethora of small groups, nongovernmental organizations, and single-issue movements have pluralized the Italian political scene, albeit unevenly from place to place.[9] Moreover, television has long been overtly politicized in Italy with the main parties previously dominating their own state channels in both personnel and message. What is perhaps most important about Berlusconi is that his almost total dominance of Italian television in recent years has helped to shape popular tastes in such a way that favor his type of celebrity political candidacy (Ginsborg 2004a; Bendicenti 2006). Even so, distracting mass publics and steering public opinion are imperfect arts, as Berlusconi's defeats in 1996 and 2006 attest. Active human agents can always react perversely to media "spin" and often match what they see on television with their own prior experience at the expense of the former (e.g., Thompson 2000, 262–3).

A second account emphasizes rather both the declining role of the regional mediation in electoral orientations alleged to have dominated Italy before 1992 and an end to the seeming rise in importance of localism and local government that took place in the 1990s and was closely associated with the political rise of the Northern League. In this construction, offered most forcefully in recent years by Ilvo Diamanti (2003a, 2003b), these old patterns are said to be giving way to a nationalized "electoral market" as "differences in votes between areas decline, the geographical gateways of single parties, those that were considered subcultures, have all faded, not only the white zone of DC but also the green zone of the League that was built and now has faded, and Democrats of the left (DS) and Reformed Communists (RC) have lost major support in the central region, above all in the districts where they were most weak in this area" (Diamanti 2003b, 239–240). In particular, "there no longer exist specific area interests that characterize the politics and the policies of the parties; above all those of the center-right, the present government. Because the majority, particularly Forza Italia, has an electoral base scattered in different zones" (Diamanti 2003b, 239). Forza Italia is characterized as practicing a "politics without territory" (Diamanti 2003a, 85). Institutionally, this trend is said to reflect a rebalancing between center and periphery, such that, for example, the 2001 election saw a ballot in which Berlusconi and his coalition were formally paired together and the national government had begun to reassert its authority as a result of EU directives and popular demands to deal with "national" problems. But this is not a return to the past, even if it is a "return of the state." To Diamanti, it is more a reimposition of authority at the center in the face of a vastly changed country in which the swing of the geographical pendulum to the periphery had gone too far.[10]

All this is particularly surprising in light of Diamanti's (2003a, 7) claim early in his book that territory qua place does not simply imply a backdrop to political processes but is "a crossroads . . . where society, politics and history are joined together and where they become visible." This is a fundamental tenet of his previous writing on Italian politics in general and the Northern League in particular. But here it has become contingent rather than necessary: present significantly only when a dominant political subject, such as the old regionally hegemonic parties in the white and red zones or the League in the far north, brings it into play. What seems to have happened is that Diamanti has fused three different conceptions of the role of territory *in* politics without clearly distinguishing their different consequences *for* Italian national politics: the role of territorial or jurisdictional claims in a party's discourse (critically that of the Northern League in relation to Padania or northern Italy versus the rest of Italy), the role of territory (or place) in social mediation between people and parties, and the relative autonomy of local politics vis-à-vis central government. The fading of either the first or the third, we would suggest, does not necessitate the fading of the other two, particularly the second, which is the primary concern of this book.

It does seem clear that the old regional subcultures, to the extent that they were ever as powerful in the regions to which they were ascribed as Diamanti alleges, have eroded. However, there is also evidence that this erosion was well under way before 1992 (Agnew 2002, Chapters 5 and 6). A case could be made for the reemergence of central state authority after a period in which it had weakened, even though big city mayors and regional governors have all acquired powers they lacked before 1992 and a watered-down devolution law giving certain health, education, and policing powers to the administrative regions passed the Italian Parliament in 2005 and came up for referendum vote in June 2006. But do trends toward a breakdown of regional party hegemonies and a reassertion of state authority necessarily signify a collapse of geographical mediation in Italian electoral politics tout court? Indeed, Diamanti's (2003a, 2003b) own empirical exposition suggests anything but. His discussion of electoral trends is entirely in terms of changing *geographies* of support. What he demonstrates, in fact, is that an idealized regional pattern has given way to a pattern of localities—or what he himself calls electoral "archipelagos" (Diamanti 2003a, 105). As the least regionalized party, Forza Italia still has a demonstrable electoral geography that, although distinctive in the precise localities it encompasses as areas of strong support, bears a remarkable geographical resemblance to the split North-South vote of the old Christian Democratic Party at the top of its game in the 1970s. At the same time, other major parties retain or have established even more definitive geographies of popular support, even as some regions have become more competitive between parties than hitherto. Even as parties have lost some of their grip on pools of support in different regions, voters still seem to exhibit distinctive patterns of electoral choice that are definitely not the same irrespective of where they are in Italy.

In idealizing an electoral past when regional party hegemonies ruled over electoral outcomes, an understandable view perhaps for someone rooted in the Italian Northeast, Diamanti has confused a dynamic and complex reterritorialization with an incipient nationalization (homogenization) of Italian electoral politics. In equating region with territory or place tout court (an almost pervasive feature of political science and history discourses about Italian society and politics) he likewise misses the extent to which geographies can take forms other than the regional. In emphasizing the role of certain parties with different roles for territory in their discourse in defining different electoral epochs and reducing each to sound-bite phrases—DC and the PCI from the 1950s to the 1980s ("politics in territory"), the League from the 1980s into the 1990s ("territory against politics"), and Forza Italia from the 1990s into the 2000s ("politics without territory")—Diamanti has also misconstrued his own evidence that electorates remain, if in different configurations over time, associated intimately with distinctively different geographical patterns of electoral choice.

More recently, Diamanti (2004) seems to explicitly backtrack from much of what he has claimed as an emerging "politics without territory." Even Forza Italia now is said to have a "territorial character" that Diamanti previously dismissed even as he described it. Indeed, the considerable losses of Forza Italia in the 2004 European and administrative elections are put down to "problems of political geography" as it lost to its national allies in their strongholds and to the center-left in many places, including Milan and Rome. Blame is laid at Berlusconi's door for relying so heavily on television and marketing, although even he is also downgraded as something of a political "has been." That Forza Italia has in fact achieved something of a foundation in many localities through colonizing chambers of commerce and more especially through its own organizational presence on the ground is still denied. Diamanti ends on a peculiar note for someone so recently enamored of "politics without territory," even as he still locates the uncertain but deterritorializing present against a past of ideological and geographical certainty when he writes: "The time of ideological fidelity and undiscussed political identities is finished: the time of eternal passions. But whoever believed that television was enough for repositioning, with marketing experts and opinion polls at the service of closed oligarchies, must reevaluate their belief. And to take up studying again: Society, territory, geography" (Diamanti 2004, 2). Of course, we couldn't agree more with this sentiment. But we think we have something in mind considerably more complex than Diamanti's vision of geography as politically homogenous regional territories that are either present or absent.

Place and Electoral Politics

We find it useful to think of explanations of political behavior as either *compositional* or *contextual* in nature (Goodin and Tilly 2006). We can offer only relatively brief remarks here about this distinction, which is the centerpiece of some recent writing on Italian politics (Agnew 2002). Compositional explanation characteristically locates behavior in individual persons and, more particularly, in their associated socioeconomic attributes but as traits not as substantial social connections. The complexities of social attachments, political reasoning, and desires are all reduced to the singular notion that unmediated individual desires determine political action (Taylor 2006). Social traits stand in as surrogates for what desires we expect different types of people to have. From this perspective, all that needs to be known about people to understand their voting and other political behaviors is which national census categories they belong to. In other words, support for political parties is best explained by reference to aggregation of the socioeconomic traits of their electorates. Contextual understanding, however, emphasizes the mediating role of social and political milieux, such as workplaces, residential and other living arrangements, party origins and organization, religious practice, immigration from distant places, and histories of social conflict, between the agency of individual persons on the one hand and making electoral choices on the other (Agnew 1987, 1996).

From this point of view, census categories are meaningless unless placed in the contexts of everyday life. The traits themselves always exist in reality as particular configurations and take on meaning and produce the reasons for why people vote they ways they do in relation to social and material attachments that are always locatable somewhere. Thus, a certain class "membership" in one context can elicit a very different meaning and, consequently, a different type of vote or party orientation than it might, for example, in a large as opposed to a small city and for the mix of people with different "generational" experiences in adolescence (this seems to be crucial in adult political socialization) in those places (e.g., Kinder 2006).

To make this point more abstractly we can use Ian Hacking's (2004, 281) turn of phrase: "Existence precedes essence." In other words, "who you are is determined by your own actions and choices" (Hacking 2004, 282), not by a priori membership in a category of a classification scheme. Classifications, however, have feedback or "looping effects" when people act as if they do belong to particular social (or other) categories. But they do so only on the basis of their own reactions to them in relation to the everyday constraints and images they experience, not because the categories define them. Consequently, "in any place and time only some possibilities even make sense" (Hacking 2004, 287).

Contexts of "place and time" are not best thought of as invariably regional, local, or national, although they frequently have elements of one, several, or all. Rather, they are best considered as always located somewhere, with some contexts more stretched over space (such as means of mass communication and the spatial division of labor) and others more localized (school, workplace, and residential interactions). The balance of influence on political choices between and among the stretched and more local contextual processes can be expected to change over time, giving rise to subsequent shifts in political outlooks and affiliations. So, for example, as foreign companies introduce branch plants, trade unions must negotiate new work practices, which, in turn, erode long-accepted views of the roles of managers and employees. In due course, this configuration of contextual changes can give an opening to a new political party or a redefined old one that upsets established political affiliations (see, e.g., on Italy, Andreucci and Pescarolo 1989; Castagnoli 2004). But changes must always fit into existing cultural templates that often show amazing resilience as well as adaptation (Griswold and Wright 2004; Cartocci 2007). Doreen Massey (1999, 22) makes the overall point most effectively when she writes: "This is a notion of place where specificity (local uniqueness, a sense of place) derives not from some mythical internal roots nor from a history of isolation—now to be disrupted by globalization—but precisely from the absolute particularity of the mixture of influences found together there."

We have used the term *place* to capture the mediating role of such geographically located milieux. What we mean by this word *place* are the settings in which people find themselves on a regular basis in their daily lives where many contexts come together and with which they may identify. Or, as it has been put previously (Agnew 2002, 21): "places are the cultural settings where localized and geographically wide-ranging socioeconomic processes that condition actions of one sort or another are jointly mediated. Although there must be places, therefore, there need not be this particular place." So, if individual persons are, in the end, the agents of politics, their agency and the particular forms it takes flow from the social stimuli, political imaginations, and yardsticks of judgment they acquire in the ever-evolving social webs in which they are necessarily enmeshed and which intersect across space in particular places (also see Baldassari 2005; Zuckerman 2005; Cartocci 2007). Mair (2006, 44) suggests that as party affiliations have weakened over the past thirty years in most European countries, voting behavior is "increasingly contingent." From our perspective, this means that geographical patterns of turnout and affiliation will become more unstable even as they often still respond to place-based (but evolving) norms of participation and differing relative attraction to the offerings of different parties.

This is a strongly sociohistorical view of politics, albeit one that also insists on the central role of spatial separations and differences in defining the concrete impacts of social influences. But such place configurations are not set in stone, so to speak. This perspective thus rejects both the extreme compositional view of electoral politics as best explained in terms of individual persons as carriers of national census attributes and the idea of fixed geographical communities in which people exercise no political agency whatsoever except as perpetuators of so-called traditional subcultural behavior. It also rejects the view that space is best thought of simply in terms of territories or spatial blocs in which regions or other spatial units are hierarchically nested, like Russian dolls, within the state territory. The absence of regional political homogeneity, for example, does not signify the absence of a political geography, only that it is constituted by a possibly richer or more variegated pattern of places that are not only separated from one another but also linked across space. From this viewpoint, therefore, if there is either a homogenization of votes for all parties across a national territory or an increased association of different parties with specific places the patterns in question (contra Caramani 2004, for example) are produced by processes that are never simply "national" or "individual" but mediated by geographical existence in webs of influence that come together through the agency of people in these places.

Post-1994 Italian Electoral Geography

The New Electoral Systems and Their Consequences

There are perhaps four preliminary points that are particularly important to note as conditioning the post-1994 electoral geography of Italy. One is that the national electorate as a whole is decreasingly linked or attached to particular parties. Even before 1992, Italian electoral mobility was substantially greater than is often alleged (Agnew 2002, 79; Pasquino 2002). Since then, mobility has increased further, creating an ever more volatile electorate. This seems to have two elements to it: a dramatic realignment of votes across parties (particularly in 1994), at least within the broadly center-left and center-right groupings, and an even more dramatic increase in abstentions or nonvoting, although this trend had begun in 1979 (Wellhofer 2001: 162–6; also see Chiaramonte, 2002; Pappalardo 2002; Natale 2006). In 2006, about one month before the election, one third of the intended voters remained undecided, according to one poll (Mannheimer 2006).[11]

A corollary of this, and a second point, is that the electoral system used from 1994 to 2001 was increasingly competitive across Italy as a whole, largely as a result of the change in the nature of the electoral system from a proportional representation (PR) to a mixed single-member district (SMD) and PR system (Bartolini et al. 2004; Ferrara 2004). Specifically, the number of single-member districts competitive between two candidates for the Chamber of Deputies increased between 1994 and 1996 by 80 percent (Reed 2001, 323). Given the high weighting of these seats in the Chamber, 475 out of 630 (155 elected by PR), the single-member element in the mixed-member majoritarian electoral system undoubtedly pushed Italy towards a bipolar system with two major electoral alliances between parties of the left and the right, respectively, and the real possibility, therefore, of alternation in national government because of the incentive it gave to preelection compacts or coalitions to reduce multiparty competition at the district level.[12] As a result, Reed (2001) finds that Duverger's Law, positing a causal relationship between single-member districts and the emergence of a two-party system, was "working in Italy." But the centralization of candidate selection within the alliances to ensure a "fair" distribution of SMDs across parties in terms of lost, marginal, and safe seats, limited the possibility of building strong ties between candidates and local constituencies. In this respect, bipolar competitiveness in Italy was bought at the expense of strong territorial representation, one of the purported benefits of SMDs. At the same time, the degree of bipolar competitiveness was not the same everywhere in Italy. As Bartolini et al. (2004) show, the South was consistently the most competitive region across the 1994, 1996, and 2001 elections with the Center as increasingly bipolar but largely noncompetitive and the North with a trend towards competitive bipolarism depending on the Northern League's relative incorporation into the House of Freedoms coalition. Even with the change back to a PR system (if one with various peculiar features, such as "topping up" the number of seats for the victorious coalition) in 2005, this geographical pattern remained much the same in the 2006 election.[13]

Across the period (and this is the third point), two coalitions organized along a basically left-right continuum have increasingly accounted for most of the votes. This undoubtedly has owed much to the political polarizing capacity of Silvio Berlusconi but is also reflected in the increasingly rightward drift of the rhetoric and policy positions of the Northern League and the recruitment into the center-left coalition of more left-wing parties (such as the Refounded Communists) hitherto outside the formal alliances.[14] The left-right distinction may well have largely disappeared elsewhere in Europe as the overriding political archetype, but in Italy it lives on powerfully in political rhetoric (e.g., (ex-) Communists still eat babies and Berlusconi is the new Mussolini) if less in terms of actual policy positions (Bobbio 1996).

Finally, as a result of these trends, focusing exclusively on the PR element in the vote for the 1994–2001 elections is particularly problematic as a singular guide to contemporary Italy's electoral geography, even though it allows for continued comparison with the pre-1993 electoral system. Yet, as Bartolini et al. (2004, 17) also point out, the new coalitions show few signs of turning into true parties in their own right. Existing party identities still seem too strong for that to happen. So, as long as a PR element exists—and it made a major comeback in the electoral system in place in 2006—the parties, including those marginal to the main coalitions, will continue to try to attract votes by running candidates, even when running them in their own right is a lost cause as far as acquiring seats in either PR or SMD contests is concerned. After all, in 2001 around 4 million voters voted for neither of the two main electoral alliances in the single-member contests. A better strategy for smaller parties under the mixed electoral system was to merge into the coalitions and maneuver for representation that way. It is clear that in this context small parties have "a large marginal value" in that they can expand the vote for coalitions (Bartolini et al. 2004, 12). But in return, they could negotiate to place their candidates in SMDs and were compensated for their alliance in coalitions by receiving more PR seats when they did not win SMD ones, thus perpetuating themselves in an alliance system (Cox and Schoppa 2002, 1050).

This brings us back to the first point. When all parties, and particularly coalitions, have weaker linkages with the electorate, bipolar competitiveness cannot be guaranteed. Voters can always defect to smaller parties or abstain completely. Although, it is important to note, the electoral system in place during the 2006 election required a very high 4 percent of total votes in order for parties to acquire seats in the Chamber of Deputies if they stayed out of the two coalitions (there was only a 2 percent requirement for parties inside the coalitions). As a result, far fewer voters strayed outside the two coalitions in 2006 than previously (Istituto Cattaneo 2006). Even so, and notwithstanding that much vote shifting involves flows of votes within voting blocs on the left and right and into and out of the electorate rather than switching between coalitions, electoral volatility, both nationally and at other geographical scales, will not soon disappear. The increasing proportion of the electorate that is actually or potentially abstention-prone is particularly important in determining the final outcome of elections, with their location being a critical factor (Mannheimer and Sani 2001; Pappalardo 2006). The more they are concentrated in relatively marginal seats, for example, the more impact they can have. As a result, the party system is not only more competitive nationally and more likely to produce governing alliances than under the First Republic but is also still favorable to the continued existence of small parties, if often within two loose coalitions.[15]

The National Elections, 1994–2006

Bearing these caveats in mind, contemporary Italian electoral geography is best examined in terms of the two "parts" of the post-1993 national elections: the SMD and PR components and the equivalent indicators emanating from the PR system adopted in 2006. With respect to the SMD component and seats/votes for the two major coalitions, the trends from 1994 to 1996, 2001, and 2006 show a fairly clear geography when, for expository purposes, the administrative regions are adopted as the units of electoral aggregation. In terms of *seats won*, the northern and southern regions are the more volatile ones overall, with the central ones being more stable. Yet, in the North and South, Lombardy, the Veneto, Friuli, Basilicata, and Sicily are exceptions to this rule in showing rather consistent affiliations to one coalition or another across all five elections, even if the Veneto "defected" in 1996 when the League stood separately from the center-right House of Freedoms (Figure 2.1). As in other majoritarian systems, it was the "swing" regions with the most marginal seats that determined the national outcome. In this regard, Piedmont, the southern peninsula regions, and Sardinia are much the most crucial regions. Overall, though, it is important to note that the electoral heft of Lombardy gave the House of Freedoms something of a head start there in accumulating SMDs even as the center-left L'Ulivo had the most consistently solid base with its hold on the central regions.

With respect to *votes cast*, rather than looking at trends by region over elections it is more useful geographically to examine trends by election over regions (Figure 2.2). This provides a visual perspective by way of a profile or transects running roughly from north (left) to south (right). For the two main coalitions, the North and Center now appear as mirror images of one another with the southern regions (except Sicily) as more similar and therefore competitive in terms of vote percentages. These graphs also reveal that votes for the two coalitions stabilized across all regions between 1996 and 2006 relative to 1994. In other words, even when noncompetitive, contests are increasingly bipolar. The transects for both sides are also increasingly shallow over time, as together they have taken a larger share of total votes relative to all parties; but there are still obvious North/Center/South differences between them. In terms of electoral outcomes, therefore, it seems clear that the center-left has much the same problem that the PCI used to have in becoming competitive away from "home" in central Italy, whereas the House of Freedoms shares the old DC problem of having to cater to such distinct constituencies as the Veneto and Lombardy, on the one hand, and Sicily on the other. Elections are still won locally, even if candidates are also still parachuted in from outside.

It is not surprising, therefore, that levels of support for different coalitions—and swings between elections to the benefit or detriment of either—differ significantly across regions. Italy is not yet socially, economically, or politically a giant pinhead with no or even limited spatial variation in its electoral geography. Geographical variance in support for the two coalitions is extremely significant in determining which one wins nationally. The enhanced role of the South in determining national electoral outcomes because of greater electoral volatility is brought into focus by the results of the 2004 European, 2005 regional, and 2006 national elections when, as Mannheimer (2004) relates for 2004, "The decisions of southern citizens are producing results ever more relevant to the political equilibrium of the entire country."

But post-1992 Italian electoral politics is not simply a recapitulation of the old PCI/DC dualism, however much the SMD component of the first three elections and the overall results at the regional level in 2006 might make it seem that way. Beneath the surface, the tectonic plates of electoral competition have been moving, particularly in the North and the South, to create different place configurations that represent a further breakdown of the regional patterns of party affiliations—these were affiliations that had generally prevailed in the 1960s and 1970s but were already under stress in the 1980s. In fact, 1992 is not, in a geographical sense, the watershed that it is often characterized as being by those of a purely historical cast of mind. The localization of Italian electoral politics

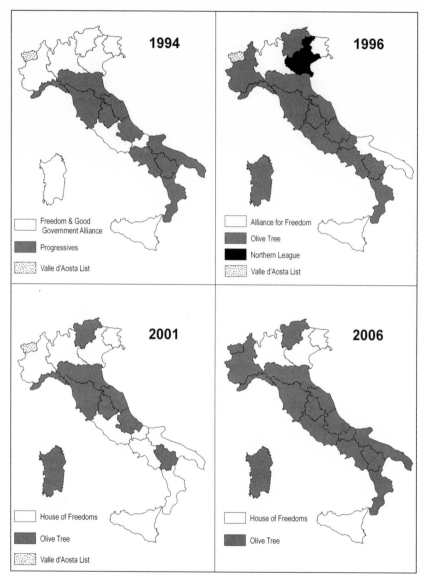

Figure 2.1 The two major electoral alliances and Italian administrative regions by overall majority of seats won, 1994–2006.

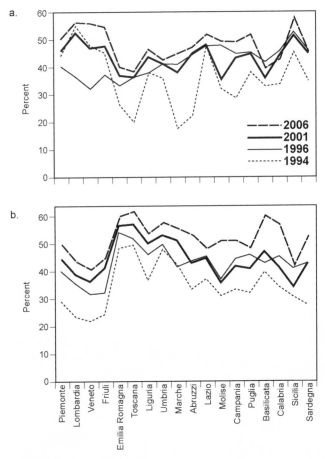

Figure 2.2 Geographical transects by administrative region (from Piemonte on the left to Sardegna on the right) of percent votes cast for: a) center-right alliance, and b) center-left alliance for 1994, 1996, 2001, and 2006 (excludes Valle d'Aosta and Trentino-Alto Adige).

was underway as early as 1979, prior to the electoral emergence of the Northern League and the collapse of the main old parties of government, the DC and PSI. The beginnings of localization were heralded in particular by the breakdown of the DC hegemony in the Northeast and the southernization of the PSI (Agnew 2002, Chapter 5).

It is the PR element of the post-1993 elections that provides the best window into the balance between old and new place configurations.[16] As Diamanti (2003a, 105) vividly describes it, this is the "geography of an archipelago." He provides a "political map of the second republic" to make his case (Figure 2.3). Of course, he is claiming that because the *zona azzurra* (blue zone) or area of strong support for Forza Italia is geographically fragmented that the map as a whole represents a "politics without territory." Presumably this is because Berlusconi (and Forza Italia) appeals to diverse constituencies that are not geographically concentrated in a single contiguous region. Putting this rather curious use of the term "territory" to one side, his general interpretive map does offer an interesting perspective on what has changed electorally since before 1992 and what has stayed the same, even if one might quibble about some of the details. The logic of this approach, with some different thresholds, can also be applied to the 2006 results (Figure 2.4) with some interesting similarities and differences.

A consolidated *zona rossa* is one of the starkest features of the maps in Figures 2.3 and 2.4, although its extent and configuration elicits little or no comment from Diamanti. The successor parties to the PCI, particularly DS and RC, have succeeded in keeping a strong regional hold even as their traditional hegemony within civil society has undoubtedly dissolved (Ramella 2005). This probably reflects the strength and competence of the parties in local government, national alliance with the Catholic-left (Margherita), the continuing importance of local-government economic regulation to local economic development, and skepticism about the expected performance of central government (see, e.g., Agnew 2002, Chapter 6; Vandelli 2002; Messina 2001). What Robert Leonardi (2003) calls "the denationalization of policy making," particularly the rising importance of elected mayors, may be especially important in underpinning the resilience of the *zona rossa* under new circumstances (see, e.g., Rampulla 1997; Magnier 2004). Not everything has changed in Italy's political configuration of places.

Yet, there is something new about the *zona rossa* of the "Second Republic," as suggested in both Figures 2.3 and 2.4. This is its

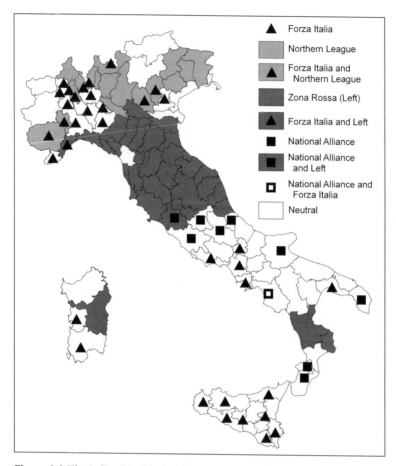

Figure 2.3 The Italian "Archipelago" according to Diamanti: PR Votes cast
in Chamber elections, 1994–2001. The "zones" are defined as sets of provinces
where a party, or in the case of the *zona rossa*, party grouping, (1) received its
largest share (top quartile) of the vote in 2001 and (2) finished first in at least
one of the three elections and second in least one other. (*Source:* Diamanti 2003a,
106.)

constitution in two segments: a still strong but attenuating central
Italian segment based around Tuscany and a potential southern one
based in Basilicata and Calabria. It is in central Italy that the economic model of small firms in industrial districts has entered into
its greatest crisis, leading perhaps to a revaluation by some voters of

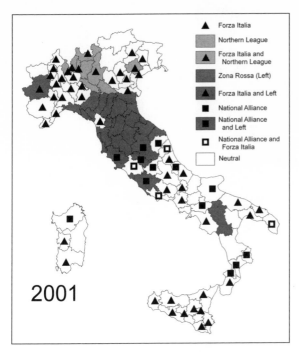

2001

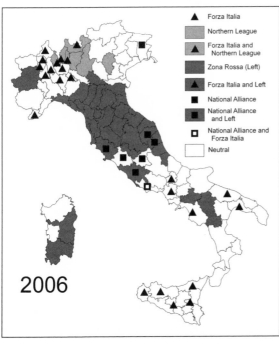

2006

Figure 2.4 The Electoral Archipelago, PR votes cast in Chamber elections, 2001 and 2006. The zones are defined as sets of provinces where parties or party groupings exceed a threshold defined as the top quartile of votes pooled across all elections (1994–2006) for the 2001 and 2006 elections. This is a more relevant definition of the relative persistence of zones than that adopted by Diamanti (2003a) and also shows provincial changes between these recent elections to illustrate the dynamism of Italy's contemporary electoral geography.

the established connection between the left-wing parties and local economic health (Agnew et al. 2005; Shin et al. 2006). Some of the poorest parts of the peninsula South in 2006 gave vote percentages for the center-left higher than those of Emilia-Romagna, signifying a distinctive shift in geographical constituency and perhaps diversification in the identities and interests of the center-left's nationwide voter base.

Of course, Forza Italia and, by 2006, a seemingly fading League have successfully colonized large parts of the North. This trend represents not only the continuing collapse of the old DC hegemony but also the rise of the class of entrepreneurs and their industrial districts that have been the source of much economic growth in the North over the past thirty years (Agnew 2002, Chapter 7; Golden 2004; Lazar 2007). The center-left has not figured out how to appeal to this electorate in national elections because it remains unattentive to the appeals for better infrastructure and lower taxes that are central to regional political discourse (Illy 2006; Panebianco 2006).[17] At the same time, it is a mistake to draw too bold a line between Forza Italia and League areas in the North, except perhaps that Forza Italia has exhibited greater support in cities, particularly in Milan; but it has recently also extended its appeal into the previous strongholds of the League. Only a populist message is likely to appeal much in the latter areas and this does not necessarily sit well with either the business orientation that Forza Italia takes in Milan or its appeal to consumerism everywhere else (see, e.g., Agnew et al. 2002; Pasquino 2003). The call of Umberto Bossi, the League's leader, during the 2006 election campaign to introduce protectionist measures to defend small northern businesses against Chinese competition, for example, is not likely to go down well with the more internationalist segments of Milan's business elite (Girardin 2006). Increasingly, however, the League has turned itself into the harder edge of Forza Italia with its government ministers from the years 2001 to 2006 often leading the charge for its other more quiescent electoral allies.[18] Thus, in practice, if not perhaps in the minds of hard-core League voters, the Northern League and Forza Italia have become more or less bonded together (Albertazzi and McDonnell 2005).

In the South all of the parties, except, for obvious reasons, the Northern League (unless, as in 2006, when it allied itself with a local notable in the province of Catania, Sicily, Raffaelle Lombardo, to garner patronage votes!) are now differentially in play. This is less so in Sicily, where Forza Italia and the UDC have a stranglehold on much of the island. Elsewhere, the geographical pattern is fragmented. There is now no single *zona meridionale*. This perhaps reflects the fact that although the South as a whole continues to experience serious economic disadvantages, no single party promises an easy resolution of its problems (e.g., Cannari and D'Alessio, 2003; Cannari and Chiri, 2004). Given that all major parties (and some minor ones) are now potentially parties of government, the historic bias of southern voters toward parties of national government now benefits none in particular. Furthermore, the different trajectories of political patronage and opinion voting in different places in the South, exposed most graphically by Simona Piattoni (1999; 2005a), suggest that different "souths" will find different parties more or less attractive depending on what is offered. The South is also less and less a single region economically, with Abruzzo and some metropolitan regions, particularly Palermo and Naples, growing at the same time other areas, such as much of Calabria, have stalled (Guerrieri and Iammarino 2006).

The *zona azzurra* as a singular "region" thus self-destructs under closer inspection. But this does not make it an example of "politics without territory." Diamanti is a victim of his own "either there is a region or there is no geography" approach to understanding of place. His Forza Italia zone is truly a congeries of places with apparently little in common save a faith in at least one of the images portrayed by Berlusconi and Forza Italia. At most, what it might suggest is that in the *zona azzurra* opinion voting (as supposedly long dominant in parts of the North) and patronage voting (held to be characteristic of the South) have found common cause in the instrumental imagery of self-serving materialism offered by Forza Italia (Piattoni 2005b).

The center-right government had successive crises in 2004–2005 largely because its components, Forza Italia and the Northern

League (the so-called northern axis), on one side, and the National Alliance and the Christian Democrat UDC, on the other, have different local and regional bases (the former in the extreme North and the Northeast, the latter in the South) and, consequently, different views about national economic and social policies (see, e.g., Diamanti and Lello 2005).[19] In particular, the more economically developed extreme North typically favors less redistributive economic policies and less intrusive social policies, whereas in the South government is a major employer and there is much greater reliance on government redistributive programs. But even within the larger regions, for example between the Center and the North, there are fundamentally different public rankings of the importance of issues such as the standard of living, public services, and criminality (Ricolfi 2005, Chapter 2). The policy differences between the parties are only at the tip of a whole set of remarkable local and regional differences in popular political attitudes across Italy that are also hardly set in geographical stone.

Conclusion

The unification of Italy is still far off, Pasquale Saraceno (1988), the famous Italian economist, averred in 1988 when discussing the economics of the southern question: why southern Italy has systematically lagged behind the north in economic development. It is still true today, electorally as well as economically and not just in terms of a north-south division. In this respect Italy is not anomalous, even if its post-1992 electoral systems may be. All countries have geographical variations in electoral outcomes. Our main conclusion in this chapter is that nationalization as a concept is often used confusingly to move from the idea of vote parallels between districts and areas in how well parties perform to the idea of causal similarity with respect to how votes are arrived at in different places. Now, nationalization can be used to describe the homogenization of votes across places over a period of time. But nationalization as deterritorialization, in the sense of politics without territory or place in its formulation, would be something else again. We hope we have shown for the Italian national elections since 1994 that "politics without territory" or place—as suggested both by those invoking the powers of television and celebrity and those claiming the emergence of a model median national voter without anything much of a standard deviation—is a slogan devoid of empirical or theoretical meaning. There may still be an Italy, in the sense of a state apparatus with a defined territorial extent, but its electoral-geographical divisibility in novel as well as historically persistent ways remains far from exhausted. Of course, this is one of the things that most fascinates many of us about Italy, notwithstanding the best efforts of those scholars and commentators who would simply turn it into a paradigm case of failed national modernity when the country refuses to live up to this or that foreign model (by not nationalizing and having other such "pathological" attributes).

3

Party Replacement, Italian Style

Much has been written about the success of Silvio Berlusconi and his party, Forza Italia. The attention that he and his party receive is indeed warranted on many levels. From his financial success and conflicts of interest to his personal appeal and public gaffes, Berlusconi is the object of both fascination and morbid curiosity. Yet *how* did Berlusconi and Forza Italia establish themselves so quickly on a political landscape once dominated by Christian Democrats, Communists, and Socialists? What exactly happened to these parties and the voters that once supported them? Was the arrival of *il Cavaliere* or "the Knight" an inevitable outcome or the confluence of a variety of very specific social, economic, political, and geographic contingencies? To understand the rise of Berlusconi's party and the recent electoral defeat of Forza Italia, it is helpful to consider how political change occurs in more general terms. As described previously in Chapter 2, it is often argued that Berlusconi epitomizes a new era in Italian politics characterized by personalities instead of political parties and by the nationalization of the electorate thanks to the psychological power of the media and the mass appeal of television. Recognizing that ballots are still cast locally, and that national averages continue to be aggregates of local outcomes, we believe that a geographical perspective can inform and extend current understandings of political change. This is the focus of this chapter. By examining how old parties, such as the Christian Democrats and the Communists, were replaced by new ones such as Berlusconi's Forza Italia and the regionalist Northern League, useful insights into political and electoral change can be obtained. Rather than seeing the geography of voting simply as a reflection of social cleavages or divisive issues (capital vs. labor, left vs. right, protectionist vs. free trade, etc.) in the electorate, on the assumption that new parties would just fill the electoral "spaces" left vacant by the old parties, we consider the geography of voting and the changes it has weathered to be diagnostic of the several sociogeographic processes by which one set of parties replaces another.

Typically, votes flow from one party or candidate to another, as well as into and out of the electorate, from one election to the next. Such vote flows are often used to explain political victories, defeats, and change. Underlying the use of vote flows to understand and explain electoral outcomes—and, more generally, political change—are two important assumptions. The first assumption is that support for parties will ebb and flow as their positions on various issues change; the second related assumption is that parties appearing on the ballot in one election will also appear on the ballot in subsequent elections. These assumptions may not be unreasonable in majoritarian electoral systems with two dominant parties, but they are certainly problematic theoretically and in relation to more complex electoral and party systems. For instance, what happens when there is a period of party-system change or in new democracies where party politics has yet to consolidate? Party systems usually disappear only with the onset of a period of dictatorship or as a result of dramatic shocks such as wars; and when they reemerge it is often in a new form as if they had been remade from scratch. After World War II countries such as Japan, France, Italy, and West Germany all went through this process. Similarly, many Central and Eastern European countries recently experienced the rebirth of party politics as part of their transition from single-party rule (Kitschelt 1992, 1995), and there are signs that fledgling party systems are even developing in places such as Iraq and the Congo.

In Italy, as in Central and Eastern Europe, the end of the cold war, which had divided post–World War II Italian politics between a dominant Christian Democratic party and the largest Communist party in the free world, combined with a corruption scandal involving the major parties of government to precipitate the collapse of the Italian party system in the early 1990s.[1] Previously, and shortly after the fall of the Berlin Wall, the leadership of the Italian Communist Party (PCI) proposed self-reform in order for the party to advance within Parliament (see Baccetti 1997; Hellman 1992; Ignazi 1992; Kertzer 1996). Support for the initiative to reform the PCI into the Democratic Party of the Left (PDS), however, was not unanimous. A small group opposed to discarding Communist ideology, which also drew support from the radical Proletarian Democracy (DP) party among other left-wing groups, splintered off to form the Refounded Communists (RC) (Foot 1996). Hence, in 1991, the left of the Italian political spectrum that was once largely occupied and dominated by the PCI, was now split between the RC and PDS.

The end of the cold war and the reconfiguration of the Italian left also removed the perceived "red" threat that the PCI had come to embody during its four decades of exclusion from government. This was significant because the success of the ruling party, the Christian Democrats, was in large part based upon its anti-Communist stance. The disappearance of the PCI effectively emancipated the Italian electorate to vote more freely, and to express its frustration with the DC's underachievement and corruption, the extent and beneficiaries of which were revealed publicly by the *Mani pulite* ("Clean Hands") and *Tangentopoli* ("Bribesville") judicial investigations of the early-1990s (see McCarthy 1997; Nelken 1996). The disintegration of the DC in 1993 is viewed as an "anticipated reaction" to the negative fallout related to the investigations into government corruption, and also resulted in the disappearance of the DC's partner in crime, the Italian Socialist Party (PSI) (Morlino 1996, 9). As notable party leaders, such as the PSI's Bettino Craxi, came under public scrutiny, others defected to create smaller parties; however, a size-able political vacuum still remained for the taking in the center of Italian politics.

The entrance of Silvio Berlusconi and his party, Forza Italia, into this political void left by the DC and PSI was unlike anything witnessed previously in Italian politics. Forza Italia's success can be attributed to its appearance with the right message at the right time, to Berlusconi's image as an outsider who was new to politics, and as described previously in Chapter 2, to his use of his three privately owned television networks. Only time would tell how astute Berlusconi would be as a politician—one with numerous conflicts of interest. Another party to emerge during this period, although it had been in existence since the early 1980s, was the regionalist Northern League (LN). Comprising various regional and local political organizations located in the northern regions of the peninsula, the Northern League and its outspoken leader, Umberto Bossi, has used particular territorial identities as their main rallying point. Over time, the language of the League has shifted back and forth from emphasizing social, economic and cultural differences between the prosperous North and public expenditure–hungry and corrupt South to the outright secession of the north that Bossi refers to as *Padania* (see Agnew 1995; Diamanti 1993, 1996). Also emerging out of the political turmoil of the early 1990s was the post-Fascist National Alliance (AN) led by Gianfranco Fini. By strategically softening its Fascist overtones, and joining forces with the more conservative elements of the now-defunct DC, the AN promoted a more democratic image and has since become an important component of Berlusconi's center-right coalition.

Political Change and Party Replacement

A period of party-system change, like that experienced in Italy in the early 1990s described above, is quite useful for empirically addressing how electoral change takes place; what might seem a reasonable assumption about the uniformity and spatial homogeneity of electoral swing in normal periods is now demonstrably open to doubt. The disruption of established partisan identifications allows for greater potential variance in the range of processes involved in how electoral change occurs. How votes flow from party to party and in and out of the electorate can no longer be presumed as geographically uniform and, analogously, as reflecting a single calculus across all voters. Answering the question of why electoral change takes place, therefore, needs a more complex understanding of how it occurs. To gain this understanding, we will examine a disruptive period such as that in Italy between 1987 and 2001.

Periods of dramatic party-system change make them ideal for examining how electoral change takes place for three reasons. First, the menu of political choice is no longer constant, so the "swing" from one party to another takes on a different meaning when the old party no longer exists or, even if still offering scattered candidates, is totally eclipsed by one or several new parties. Second, new parties may not necessarily represent the same cleavages, divisions, or issues upon which support for the old parties rested, so it cannot be presumed that replacement simply involves switching from a single old party to a single new one. Finally, new parties might concentrate their electoral efforts in different places from the old ones by "specializing" regionally or picking certain targeted demographic, social, and cultural constituencies for particular attention, including groups hitherto shunned or ignored.

Although there is a tradition of research on party organization and party change (e.g., Janda 1980; Katz and Mair 1994; Panebianco 1988), relatively little has been written on the specific outcomes of transitions between party systems and, more specifically, on how such transitions are navigated in electoral terms. Such periods are relatively rare, particularly when wars and periods of dictatorship are excluded; but they do occur and there are analogies between them and situations of dramatic electoral change involving third parties and large vote swings between previously dominant parties. The "remaking" of existing major parties in the United States and United Kingdom has also taken attention away from cases where new parties spring up to replace long-established ones. Moreover, the cleavage and rational-choice models of political behavior would both predict a tendency for replacement to be synonymous with substitution. Both perspectives see political expectations in terms of relatively fixed political-issue "spaces" in which the various dimensions of political choice (left/right, Catholic/anticlerical, etc.) are given. Consequently, new parties will tend to slot into electoral space more or less as substitutes for the ones that have left. This is a problematic presumption because party replacement is not exhausted by substitution.

Types of Party Replacement

The central question of this chapter concerns how the term *replacement* is understood with regard to political change. One party replacing another in electoral competition can be thought of in terms of a number of understandings of the term *replacement*. In one meaning *replacement* is akin to *substitution* when the new party takes over all or a large share of the votes of a previous one that has disappeared. This is the quantitative electoral sense in which the term is used by most commentators. In another related understanding, however, *replacement* involves a number of parties *splitting* an old party's votes among themselves. In a third scenario, the collapse or disappearance of one party draws attention to a crisis in the social world that the old party had long represented. This allows an existing, opportunistic party to move in and *colonize* that world, not necessarily by taking over the old vote so much as providing a voice for and *mobilizing* new voters and elements increasingly alienated from the old party even before its final disappearance.

This third understanding of the term *replacement* draws particular attention to three important theoretical premises when thinking about how new parties achieve support as old ones disappear. These premises are geographical. This is why understanding *replacement* means understanding its geographical forms. One premise is that electoral choices should be seen in relation to the discrete *social-territorial settings* or places in which such choices are exercised. Old parties do not simply disappear for no reason even when they "rot from the head down," i.e., disintegrate organizationally before they disappear in electoral terms. Often they are no longer in tune with local social mores, and their electoral persistence is more a matter of inertia than persisting enthusiasm from a popular base. New issues such as the environment, foreign immigration, globalization, and women's rights create new constituencies and divide populations in new ways. But choices made also reflect the choices available. These are a function of candidate lists, the strength of party organization, campaign strategies, and local issues feeding into ones of wider relevance upon which parties run for election.

Second, parties are not simply electoral vehicles, although orthodox thinking in Anglo-American political science often regards them as such, perhaps because the American parties (as opposed to individual representatives) often seem unrelated to particular population or sectional interests. Parties can be more or less effective *intermediaries between state and society*, channeling resources from center to periphery and rewarding some social and territorial interests at the expense of others. In this sense the distinction between mass parties and patronage parties is a false dichotomy: all parties are patronage parties. Judgments are made about how effective the party is in "delivering the goods" and whether or not we (in our place) are being rewarded more or less than they (in their place). Much of the geography of party politics is a result of who gets what (and when and where they get it) than a reflection of "underlying" or foundational social cleavages that have a geographical bias to them.

Third, new parties can have totally different *symbolic, interest, and strategy repertoires* from the parties they replace. In particular, they can appeal to new *territorial formulations* of the dilemmas that the old party dealt with through allocations of public resources (Agnew 1997). Ethnic and regionalist parties are the most obvious exponents of such a territorialized approach. Typically they focus on regional relative deprivation or a sense of resentment at the relative success of other regions in commanding state resources or acquiring more than an average per capita share of national revenues. But nationalist parties wanting to expel foreigners and put up protectionist barriers and liberal parties desiring to remove all limits on trade and investment are also engaged in territorial reframing.

Since we consider party replacement to be an intrinsically geographic process, an explicitly geographic perspective is necessary to disentangle the types of replacement identified above. Votes are indeed channeled between parties from one election to the next, and though it may be convenient to view such electoral change as geographically invariant, such flows are seldom uniform across any democracy. Therefore, in order to completely understand electoral change it is necessary to elucidate how it occurs.

The Spatial Analysis of Party Replacement

Particularly useful is a technique that is sensitive to the processes underlying party replacement—one that recognizes electoral change as not being regulated by a singular logic arbitrarily and uniformly applicable across all territorial units. In certain circumstances, there may be no direct relationship between old and new parties, in other situations one or more parties may be the direct descendents of a disappeared party, and still other cases may reveal that electoral flows to a new party tend to vary considerably across Italy. The ability to distinguish between different types of party replacement (i.e., colonization/mobilization, vote splitting and substitution) and levels of political change in Italy indicates the need to frame politics geographically.

In order to differentiate between the various types of party replacement, and to evaluate political change in Italy, we use a spatial analytic framework. Spatial analysis is premised upon the fact that spatially referenced data are "special" (Anselin 1989; Haining 2003; O'Sullivan and Unwin 2003). Spatially or geographically referenced data refer to data that are collected on the basis of identifiable locations or places, such as census enumeration units, electoral precincts or in this case Italian provinces and *comuni* or municipalities. What makes spatial data special is that the data collection units are correlated geographically, and values of individual observations are thus correlated with each other and not independent as classical probability theory necessitates. The geographic concentration or local clustering of similar values in a data set is formally called spatial autocorrelation, or spatial dependence. Premised upon what is referred to as Tobler's first law of geography, which states that everything is related but closer things are more related than distant things, most georeferenced data exhibit some degree of spatial autocorrelation (Tobler 1963). The presence of spatial dependence, for example, in the dependent variable of a regression equation, may result in biased and inconsistent parameter estimates, and subsequently, incorrect inferences (Anselin 1988). In other words, borrowing from the classic work by Peter Gould (1970) on the topic of geographical statistics, failure to consider and account for spatial autocorrelation makes statistical inference the "geographical name for a wild goose."

Within electoral studies, spatial analysis and geographic methodologies are gaining recognition as useful, if not always necessary, techniques (e.g., Calvo and Escolar 2003; Kim et al. 2003). As an increasing amount of geo-referenced election data become available, researchers are increasingly aware of both the opportunities and implications that come from working with spatial data. For instance, theories of voting that consider sociogeographic processes (e.g., diffusion of politically relevant information, neighborhood effects) and place-based structures (e.g., social networks, institutions) that bias political information and behavior can benefit from spatial analytic methods. In addition to the detection and evaluation of spatial autocorrelation in Italian election data[2], we show how spatial analysis can be used to examine electoral change, and to disentangle and clarify how old parties were replaced by new ones across Italy.

Table 3.1 provides a comparative overview of support for old and new parties between 1987 and 2001. The vertical arrangement of parties mimics the span of the Italian political spectrum with left-wing parties placed in the topmost rows, centrist parties in the middle and right-wing parties in the bottom rows. The "Other" category aggregates the support for parties across the political spectrum that received less than five percent of the total vote. A casual analysis of Table 3.1 indicates that there is not a direct correspondence between the old parties that appeared on the ballot in 1987 and 1992 and the new parties that replaced them in subsequent

TABLE 3.1   VOTE SHARES FOR ITALIAN POLITICAL PARTIES, 1987–2001.

	1987	1992	1994	1996	2001
	Old party system		New party system		
Italian Communist Party (PCI)	26.6				
Refounded Communists (RC)		5.6	6.0	8.6	5.0
Democratic Party of the Left (PDS)		16.1	20.4	21.1	16.3
Daisy Party (MRG)					14.3
Italian Socialist Party (PSI)	14.3	13.6			
Christian Democrats (DC)	34.3	29.7			
Forza Italia (FI)			21.0	20.6	29.1
Northern League (LN)		8.7	8.4	10.1	4.1
National Alliance (AN)			13.5	15.7	11.9
Italian Social Movement (MSI)	5.9	5.4			
Other	18.9	21.0	30.7	24.0	19.2

elections. Therefore, a more complex or nuanced understanding of the concept of replacement needs to be considered.

Determining whether or not, and to what extent, the geography of support for the new parties overlaps the historical strongholds of old parties may also serve to illustrate how the process of party replacement is geographically contingent. Figure 3.1 maps provincial levels of support for the Italian Communist Party (PCI), the Christian Democrats (DC), and Italian Social Movement (MSI) the last time that each appeared on the ballot. The center of the peninsula, with its high concentration of PCI support is often referred to as the "red zone" or "red belt." Conversely, the northeast of Italy, long recognized as a stronghold for the Christian Democrats, was once referred to as the "white zone." It is well established that levels of electoral support for the new and the old political parties in Italy exhibit varying degrees of local clustering as well as regional diversity (see Agnew et al. 2002; Brusa 1984; Cartocci 1990; Diamanti and Mannheimer 1994; Galli and Prandi 1970; Shin and Agnew 2002; Agnew 2002). These geographic clusters and variations are clearly evident in Figure 3.1, and can in part be attributed to spatial processes that rely upon the interdependence of places (Haining 2003). Spatial processes such as diffusion, exchange and transfer, interaction, and dispersal are frequently manifested as spatial autocorrelation in quantitative data, which at the

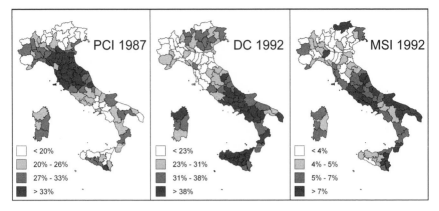

Figure 3.1 Geographic distribution of support for the Italian Communist Party (1987), Christian Democrats (1992), and Italian Social Movement (1992).

local scale may reflect information networks, the spatial (re)-organization of political parties or any number of social, economic, cultural, and/or political interactions or exchanges. The processes that contribute to such local clustering also account for the geographic variation in electoral support and in changes at the regional and national levels (e.g., Johnston and Pattie 1992; Pattie and Johnston, 1997). The theoretical argument underlying such regional variations is that voters mediate and respond to myriad social, economic, and political processes that influence political attitudes and behavior differently in different places (Agnew 1987a; Johnston 1986, 1992).

To formally evaluate regional clusters and variations in electoral support, such as those illustrated in Figure 3.1, we need to determine whether or not support in one location is related to support in neighboring locations. One way to compare the value of a location to its neighbors is to calculate a spatially lagged variable (Anselin 1992).[3] The spatial lag is in effect the weighted average of values that surround any given observation. Used in many statistical indicators of spatial association, such as Moran's I, spatially lagged variables provide a simple way to capture and to summarize geographic relationships in quantitative data. For instance, a statistically significant, positive value of Moran's I indicates the presence of spatial depend-

TABLE 3.2 MORAN'S I SCORES FOR SELECTED OLD AND NEW PARTIES, 1987–2001. ALL VALUES ARE SIGNIFICANT AT THE $P < 0.001$ LEVEL.

	1987	1992	1994	1996	2001
	Old party system		New party system		
Italian Communist Party (PCI)	0.70				
Refounded Communists (RC)		0.70	0.80	0.60	0.50
Democratic Party of the Left (PDS)		0.73	0.72	0.72	0.69
Daisy Party (MRG)					0.25
Christian Democrats (DC)	0.53	0.71			
Forza Italia (FI)			0.74	0.58	0.37
Northern League (LN)		0.75	0.72	0.72	0.59
National Alliance (AN)			0.80	0.69	0.58
Italian Social Movement (MSI)	0.43	0.50			

ence, and a significant negative value suggests a pattern of dissimilarity. Moran's I values for a sampling of parties from the old and in the new Italian party system are reported in Table 3.2.

Values of Moran's I for all parties are positive and highly significant, indicating that electoral support for each party of interest is not distributed randomly across the Italian peninsula. When comparing levels of clustering between old and new parties, or over time, both continuities and variations are identifiable. For example, there is a certain degree of continuity, at least initially, in the value of Moran's I for parties of the left (i.e., PCI, [P]DS, RC and MRG), but with each subsequent election, values decrease and move farther away from the value associated with the PCI. Similar trends exist for the Christian Democrats (DC) and what are considered its primary replacements, Forza Italia (FI) and the Northern League (LN). Finally, support for the post-Fascist National Alliance (AN) appears to be more clustered than for its predecessor the Italian Social Movement (MSI). Notwithstanding assumptions, correct or incorrect, about which new parties replaced old ones, electoral support for all parties of interest is significantly clustered in each election.

Given the overview of the recent crisis of the Italian party system, and the fact that electoral support for most parties in both the old and new Italian party system is spatially dependent (see Table 3.2), there is reason to expect that spatiotemporal relations exist between votes for the old and the new parties. Conversely, since replacement arguably is not a singular process, or one that is completely explained by direct substitution, an approach that can elucidate how replacement is played out across the Italian peninsula, in different locations, is constructive. The next section provides a worked example and shows how spatial analysis can be used to locate areas and regions of spatiotemporal stability and instability, which in turn reveal the possible sociogeographic processes that underlie party replacement in Italy.

The Replacement of the Christian Democrats in the Veneto and Italian Communists in Tuscany

As noted earlier, since World War II the Italian party system has exhibited a strong regional pattern of support for different political parties. This regionalization of support reflects a range of influences such as historical differences in local societies, the origins of political parties in different places, and the economic attributes of different localities (e.g., Trigilia 1986; Baccetti 1997; Shin 2001; Lucani 1989; Agnew 2002). But it also illustrates the ease with which parties with regional bases of support can prosper under proportional representation. From the late 1940s through the 1970s no two regions of Italy showed greater specificity with respect to dominance by particular political parties than the Northeast and the Center, the former with Christian Democrats (DC) and the latter with the Italian Communist Party (PCI). Indeed, the extent to which the Catholic DC dominated the Northeast and the PCI the Center led them to be labeled, respectively, as the "white" and "red" zones not just because of relative electoral success but also because of the reinforcement of affiliated organizations that gave the parties a social role well beyond that of typical party politics (Messina 1997; Agnew 2002, Chapter 5) (refer to Figure 3.1).

Although these regional hegemonies showed signs of fraying before the final collapse of the party system in 1992, the parties' regional dominance remained substantial until the end (Agnew 2002, Chapter 5). However, what has replaced them is quite different in the two areas. In the Northeast, new parties without a religious or ideological link to what they have replaced, in particular the regionalist Northern League (LN) and the new center-right party Forza Italia, have more or less taken the place of DC as the main parties. This is an entirely new political configuration for this area of Italy. In the second case, two new parties emerged out of the party that disappeared: the Democratic Party of the Left (PDS) and the Refounded Communists (RC). This can be thought of as a split in an existing party more than the replacement of an old party by entirely new ones, but it is important to emphasize that neither PDS nor RC is a simple substitute for the old PCI.

To illustrate the geographical dynamics underlying party replacement, we focus on how the Northern League replaced the Christian Democrats across the Veneto and how the PDS replaced the Communists in Tuscany. To assess whether or not there is indeed a degree of geographical continuity between old and new parties, we first compare the levels of clustering for the parties of interest, the DC and PCI from the old party system and the LN and PDS in the new one. Such comparisons provide preliminary insights into the nature of the geography of party replacement. Tuscany and the Veneto serve as relevant examples because it is often presumed that the process of replacement was more or less dominated by only one "new" party in each region, although the origins of each new party are quite different. Such a comparison further illustrates the need to identify geographic differences in electoral change and highlights the fact that replacement connotes diverse sets of processes for different parties as well as for different places. Similar levels of spatial dependence between the old and new parties would suggest that the new party inherited some of the geographic bases of support, or it overlaps the social, political, and geographic milieu of the old party. Dissimilar levels of spatial dependence indicate the possibility of a change in the electoral geography of the region, marked by the disappearance of one party and the emergence of another. In this case, the new party may occupy or colonize completely different social, political, and economic groups and rely upon different sets of information networks and modes of spatial organization.

Using municipal level data, Table 3.3 reports Moran's I values for the parties of interest in our worked example. Note that the DC and LN competed against each other until the 1994 election when the former party disintegrated, therefore, prereplacement Moran's I scores for both parties are provided for comparison. A Moran's I score of 1.0 indicates perfect spatial autocorrelation, or that each observation can effectively be predicted by the average of surrounding observations. During the replacement phases, the period between 1987 and 1992 from the PCI to PDS and the period between 1992 and 1994 from the DC to LN, Moran's I values slightly increase. Scores for both the PDS and LN are also above those of the party they arguably replaced in each and every election. The similarity of Moran's I values for the PCI and PDS in Tuscany suggest that the latter may have inherited many territorial bastions of support; but in the Veneto, the fact that LN support is more geographically concentrated than that of the disappeared DC indicates the League may not have been a universal substitute for the once-dominant Catholic party.

To obtain more detailed insights into party replacement, a local indicator of spatial association (LISA), the local Moran statistic, can also be used.[4] Unlike the global Moran's I index which returns a single value for an entire data set, local Moran values are calculated for each individual observation, or in this case, each municipality. Local Moran's I statistics provide information about the degree and nature of clustering around each observation by determining the "contribution" that each observation makes to the overall global statistic. In fact, the average of local Moran's I statistics is equivalent to the global Moran's I value. Since a local Moran's I index is calculated for each observation, values can be plotted or mapped to identify positive spatial dependence (i.e., high values surrounded by similarly high values, or low values surrounded by similarly low values), or spatial outliers (i.e., high values surrounded by low values, or low values surrounded by high values).

Complementing the local Moran's I statistic is the bivariate version of the statistic. The equation for the bivariate LISA is identical

TABLE 3.3   MORAN'S I SCORES FOR THE DC, LN, PCI, AND PDS
IN THE VENETO AND TUSCANY, 1987–1996. ALL VALUES ARE
SIGNIFICANT AT THE *P* < 0.001 LEVEL.

	1987	1992	1994	1996
	Old party system		New party system	
The Veneto (N=582)				
Christian Democrats (DC)	0.65	0.52		
Northern League (LN)		0.78	0.84	0.83
Tuscany (N=287)				
Italian Communist Party (PCI)	0.64			
Democratic Party of the Left (PDS)		0.67	0.72	0.69

to the local Moran, but a different variable is used for the spatial lag
component. In this example and in subsequent analyses, the spatial
lag component is the respective mean deviated level of support for
the old parties of interest the last time that each appeared on the ballot. Hence, the bivariate LISA serves as a diagnostic for evaluating
the geography of party replacement. More precisely, the bivariate
LISA permits the identification and visualization of four types of
spatiotemporal correlation:

I. High levels of support for new party *z* surrounded by
   high levels of support for old party *y*; is consistent with
   switching and possibly the splitting of votes between two
   or more parties;
II. low levels of support for new party *z* surrounded by high
   levels of support for old party *y*; suggests the new party is
   unable to colonize areas where old party *y* once enjoyed
   success;
III. low levels of support for new party *z* surrounded by low
   levels of support for party *y*; is consistent with a certain
   degree of spatiotemporal stability, like type I above;
IV. high levels of support for party *z* surrounded by low levels
   of support for party *y*, suggests that the new party may be
   mobilizing a new segment of voters or colonizing areas
   where the old party was weak.

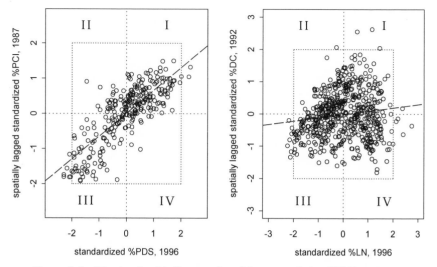

Figure 3.2   Bivariate local indicators of spatial autocorrelation (LISA) scatterplots between the PCI 1987 and PDS 1996 in Tuscany (left) and the DC 1992 and the LN 1996 (right).

The question at hand is this: "To what extent is the new party's support related to the historic and geographic support of the party it replaced?" When visualized on a scatterplot, observations falling in either quadrant I or III denote the clustering of similarly high or low values, and observations in quadrants II and IV indicate spatial dissimilarities (see Figure 3.2).

Figure 3.2 plots the relationship between the PCI in 1987 and the PDS in 1996 within Tuscany, and the relationship between the DC in 1992 and the LN in 1996 within the Veneto. At the regional level, the spatiotemporal process of replacement is very different in Tuscany when compared to that in the Veneto. The plot on the left confirms that the PDS is the primary replacement of the PCI, probably drawing support from the PCI's long-established electoral strongholds. Returning a bivariate Moran's I value of 0.65, historically above average support for the PCI in surrounding communities is related to below average support (i.e., quadrant II) for the PDS in only thirty-seven of the 287 cases. Within the Veneto plot on the right, the number of observations is distributed fairly evenly between quadrants. The patterns, or lack thereof, and a weak bivariate Moran's I value of only 0.10 indicate that in many places, LN support is positively related to historic levels of DC support (54 percent of cases), but in other areas, the relationship is negative. Specifically, some areas that once supported the DC do not seem to support the LN at comparable levels, and in some areas where support for the DC was relatively weak, the LN has made notable inroads. This suggests that in some places in the Veneto, the LN did substitute for the DC, but in others that mobilizations of new and old non-DC voters outside of DC strongholds was the main feature of the transition.

Conclusion

We contend that party replacement is not equivalent to substitution and can involve a diverse array of geographical processes. Moreover, the electoral processes underlying party replacement are geographic in nature. For instance, it is often presumed that the Northern League replaced the Christian Democrats throughout northern Italy, and in some places this is indeed what occurred. However, our municipal-level spatial analyses reveal that while the League was able to attract former DC voters and to colonize some provinces of the Veneto, it was also a poor choice relative to other possible DC replacements, such as Forza Italia. We also show how the Democratic Party inherited most (but not all) of the vote for the former-Italian Communist Party (PCI) across Tuscany. Both examples illustrate clearly how the process of replacement can be more complex than the direct substitution of one party for another.

Explanations for the popularity of the League, and in particular, its ability to colonize new "spaces" in the Veneto are, in part, linked to increasing levels of secularization in the region and the failure of the DC to support the local small firms and enterprises that are credited with bolstering the Italian economy over the last quarter century (Riccamboni 1997, 299). The stagnating and corrupt DC model of representation, which relied upon small towns and rural agricultural areas, failed to recognize and address the needs of the growing northern Italian economy that was characterized by high levels of employment, rising productivity, and industrialization (Diamanti 1993). It is precisely in the industrial districts and the "urbanized countryside" of the North where the League's platform based upon *localismo*—or the preservation, promotion, and protection of local territorial identities and culture— resonated the most with voters.

Our discussion about party replacement and the implementation of spatial analysis illustrates the need to consider the geographical bases of political change. The detection of spatial clustering is important when examining and explaining political change because it is often presumed that political change is a stationary process. For instance, when using flow of vote estimates to evaluate political changes at the national level, it is implied that vote shifts between parties are consistent in magnitude and direction across all units of analysis, and consequently, that units of analysis are more or less identical and interchangeable with one another (Agnew 1996). This assumption is often untenable, and in some cases it may be problematic because electoral shifts are likely to be either underestimated or overestimated, depending upon where they are obtained. In other words, political change is seldom uniform across a single country. Therefore, using spatial analysis prior to obtaining estimates of vote flows and voter transitions may improve estimates and yield a more accurate account of electoral change. In the next chapter we show how electoral change occurs and locate precisely such changes in order to obtain a historical understanding of the rise and fall of Berlusconi (more specifically, his party, Forza Italia, and the center-right coalition that he has headed since 1994).

4

The Geographical Secret to
Berlusconi's Success

O
f course, Berlusconi's political career as head of a center-right coalition would never have been possible but for the collapse of the old parties and the electoral system associated with them. At the same time, the new electoral system, introduced after public approval in a referendum in 1993, definitely encouraged the emergence of clear groupings of parties because of the overwhelming importance of the majoritarian element (the 75 percent of seats in the Chamber and the Senate awarded in single-member districts that would reward larger electoral coalitions) in the new system (see Chapter 2). The critical question from our point of view, which emphasizes the geography of electoral affiliations, is how Berlusconi was able to create and make workable the center-right coalition beginning in February 1994 and extending through, if with considerable difficulty along the way, the years 1995 to 2000 in particular, up until his narrow defeat of 2006.

The focus of this chapter, therefore, is chiefly on the elections of 1994 and 2001, because these were the successful ones for Berlusconi's coalition; but this chapter also focuses to a degree on the politics of coalition-building, particularly why the center-right was more successful at this activity earlier than its putative opponents and how the coalition came back together again in light of its seeming disintegration, after the defection of the Northern League, between 1995 and 2000. The point is not to deny the role of the persona and anomalous institutional position of Berlusconi as Italy's richest man (in the later years of his term in office, at least) and owner of its three main private television channels in making the coalition possible but to strongly suggest that other factors have also been at work in putting this coalition together, not least of which was the electoral system of 1993 and the evolving peculiarities of Italian electoral geography (see Chapter 2).

We begin with a discussion of how Berlusconi created Forza Italia in 1993–94 and then organized a geographically disparate coalition through *separate* alliances with the nationalist/recently Fascist AN in the South and the regionalist Northern League in the North. Together Forza Italia and the League colonized former Christian Democrat voters and mobilized new ones in the North. AN substituted for the old Fascist MSI especially strongly in parts of the peninsula South. We note how this conjunction unraveled with the defection of the League in 1995 and how the 1996 election was more a defeat for Berlusconi than a victory for the center-left. The center-left, however, was an even more unstable enterprise because of the ideological divisions between the heirs of the former PCI and the difficulties of incorporating the Catholic left (former DC voters), and others, into the coalition. During the years in opposition, with the League largely now hostile to Berlusconi, there seemed limited possibility of recreating the successful formula of 1994 of the alliances between Forza Italia and the League in the North and between Forza Italia and the AN in the South. Yet, in 2000 Berlusconi succeeded in doing this and establishing a much more integrated center-right coalition than had existed previously. Some of the impetus for the rapprochement was the result of the poor performance of the League and the AN in previous administrative and European elections. But more was due to a "compact" between Berlusconi and Bossi, leader of the League, promising to pursue Bossi's vision of "devolution" for northern Italy. This revival of the coalition around a Berlusconi-Bossi axis is an important part of the story of the "Berlusconi years," and along with the center-left's disastrous campaign, produced the landslide victory for the center-right in 2001—the true beginning of Berlusconi's time in the sun. This victory rested partly on increased success for the center-right as a whole in the North and Sicily (where Forza Italia was successful largely on its own) but also more crucially on a significant expansion of support in the peninsula South into a relatively large number of relatively marginal seats. But this geographical pattern would come back to haunt the center-right coalition in 2006, notwithstanding Berlusconi's media control and ability as prime minister to manipulate some political events to his advantage with perhaps the ultimate coup de grace coming in the constitutional referendum of June 2006 with its massive defeat for the devolution proposal that had brought Berlusconi and Bossi together in 2000 (see Chapter 6).

Forza Italia and the Making (and Breaking) of the Center-Right, 1994–1999

The political significance of the *Tangentopoli* scandal of 1992 lay in the inability of existing parties to recover their reputations from the serious crimes to which it drew attention while remaining organizationally unchanged. The PCI had already broken up in 1991 as much in response to the end of the cold war as to Italian domestic pressures; this removed the main "threat" that had kept DC together in the face of previous scandals and challenges. The PSI, and its leader Bettino Craxi, were at the heart of the scandal and thus incapable of providing an alternative fulcrum around which a renewed party system could coalesce. The scandal of illegal party financing was therefore crucial, directly and indirectly, in undermining the legitimacy and organization of most of the existing parties across the political spectrum. Quickly it became clear that the only ways out of the impasse into which the parties had fallen were either to organize new parties or repackage old ones. Only the old MSI and the

Northern League survived from before 1992, the former rapidly mutating into the "post-Fascist" national Alliance under its leader Gianfranco Fini, and the latter became a relatively new alliance of the various Leagues in northern Italy dominated by the figure of Umberto Bossi, leader of the Lombard League.

As suggested in Chapter 2, between 1976 and 1992 there had already been significant erosion in electoral support for the largest parties relative to the rise in popular support for various "protest" parties such as the League and the Greens and a revived PSI. In 1976 fully 73.1 percent of the vote for the Chamber of Deputies went to DC and the PCI; but by 1987 this had fallen to 60.9 percent. And in 1992 DC and the two main heirs to the PCI (PDS and Refounded Communists) accounted for only 51.4 percent of the vote for the Chamber. So, if *Tangentopoli* was the defining moment for the final demise of the old system, the two largest parties had already begun losing their electoral centrality long before. The end of the cold war, the failure of DC to respond adequately to the demands of its historic constituency of small businesses in the Northeast, and the relative breakdown of the Communist and Catholic political subcultures (particularly the Catholic one) all seem to have played some role in this loss of centrality.

One particularly dynamic force in the later years of the old party system had been Craxi's PSI which had achieved some success, largely through its garnering of votes in the South and in and around Milan, as an alternative to DC. The PSI, notwithstanding its travails in 1992–1993, provided something of a model for how at least one part of the political spectrum, that most devastated by *Tangentopoli*, could be reorganized. It had long lost its connotation as an ideological leftist party. Since becoming party secretary in 1976, Craxi had turned it into a "middle" party, in Hazan's (1996) sense, attempting to make the party a pivotal element in the center-ground of Italian politics but without a strong ideological commitment to traditional political centrism (secularism, civil rights, liberal economics, etc.). It appealed particularly to an Italian social grouping that can be thought of in terms of a threatened political identity as much or more than in terms of defense of specific political interests.

This grouping would be those most invested in the political exchange relationships and corporative ties (fueled by everything from kickbacks and bribes for government contracts to the lack of enforcement of laws and rules governing land use and tax collection) in which control over the state was necessary in order to maintain freedom of action in much more important private social and economic relationships.[1] Reinforcing this outlook was the increased importance of personal consumption and the decline of religion and political ideology as elements of self-definition since the 1970s (Cartocci 1990; Ricolfi 1994). In Bodei's (2006, 142) words: "an ethics based more on unrestrained individual preferences took precedence over an ethics based on norms which were imposed by tradition, religion, or the search for the 'common good.' "[2]

This political orientation involved not just those favored directly by possible government policies but also those looking to the state *not* to do anything that would negatively affect the incomes, consumption, and decisions of their group, family, clientele, or community.[3] Italy has a vast population of self-employed people, on the one hand, and many government employees, on the other, whose social self-definition is all about maintaining a particularistic relationship with one another and with the politicians who represent them. They are conservative in the sense of wishing to be left alone by government except insofar as it is advantageous for them personally or as part of some grouping to benefit from government largesse. This is what is meant by the culture of *raccomandazione*, or use of public roles and connections for private ends. Such people had historically supported DC and, increasingly, the PSI. They were still available for renewed representation once the immediate hysteria of the corruption scandals over party financing and insider dealing had faded away.[4] Their identities as Italians, members of this or that interest group, consumers, or nostalgia for an authoritarian past might differ from place to place and thus with respect to which parties they would prefer (see Chapter 2).

But control over government to conserve their social position, not adherence to a reforming ideology (such as, say, neoliberalism or increased privatization of state assets and increased openness of the

Italian economy), lay at the center of this grouping's political agenda. Indeed, a strong case can be made that since 1992 the Italian center-left has been much more oriented toward reform of both state and society, not least in using the former for the latter, including policies of a neoliberal disposition (see, e.g., Perna 2006; Alesina and Giavazzi 2007).[5] Although Berlusconi and his allies, particularly the League, might use the rhetoric of diminishing the powers of government and unleashing entrepreneurial energy, what actually joined them to the more obviously statist AN was commitment to a big-government conservatism in which, rather like the Reagan administration in the United States, tax cuts and legitimizing tax avoidance would be combined with the use of government to serve those components of society whose incomes depended on favorable (or absent) regulation, government employment or subsidy, and the monopoly rents from government-sanctioned activities (as with Berlusconi's own media business). Of course, this common set of orientations did not guarantee agreement about either policies or personnel. In particular, the North-South divide over the role of central government apparent between the Northern League, on the one hand, and the AN, on the other, was to bedevil the center-right throughout the 1990s.

Berlusconi was very much the most important of the people committed to the culture of *raccomandazione*, having been largely dependent on his connections with Craxi and the PSI for his acquisition of the three private TV channels he controlled and for covering his financial tracks in other areas, such as his Milan real estate operations (Stille 2006). He quickly saw the danger to his own future if a resurgent center-left won national office and set about limiting his economic freedom of action. He also saw that the new largely majoritarian electoral system, introduced after a popular referendum in 1993, was designed to encourage coalition formation by parties before elections and to avoid the ministerial horse-trading and government insecurity after elections of the old PR system; therefore, he knew this would require him to find congenial electoral partners to lower the risk of "going it alone" with his own party. There are, therefore, two parts to the story of Berlusconi's entry into Italian national politics: the creation of his own political party, Forza Italia, which has acquired the lion's share of attention, and the construction of an alliance with other parties to put together an electoral coalition, which has received considerably less attention, but is arguably just as important.

Apparently it was Craxi who, in April 1993, "seeing that his own days in power were numbered" (Stille 2006, 132), first suggested to Berlusconi that he become actively involved in national politics. He saw the potential magic in combining Berlusconi's media power with the anti-Communist vote that seemingly had nowhere to go with the dissolution of DC and the PSI. Only when the Milan prosecutors began to turn their attention to Fininvest, Berlusconi's holding company, for its questionable involvements in the old regime did Berlusconi actively begin to consider founding his own political party. From the outset, he thought of this in the context of providing a focus for the center-right as a whole rather than as an independent force in itself (Stille 2006, 135). In this view, aligned closely with that of Craxi, through proper marketing and "product placement" and drawing from his business experience, Berlusconi could provide a fulcrum for a reorganization of political forces on the center-right to keep out the seemingly ascendant forces of the left whose main advantage was the superior organization of the main heir of the PCI, the PDS. Initially, he was drawn to considering such figures as Mario Segni, the architect of the electoral reform, or Mino Martinazzoli, the leader of the largest party emanating from the wreckage of DC (the PPI), as candidates for whom he could serve as an éminence grise. But if Segni was repulsed by the potential need, as Berlusconi saw it, to bring either or both the post-Fascists and Northern League into any successful alliance, Martinazzoli also rejected the "middle party" strategy as salesmanship more than politics as he understood it. Private polling on his behalf and a summer spent watching the political talk shows on Italian TV (1993), finally led Berlusconi to choose an all-too-appropriate name for a new party that he would himself head. The name he chose, Forza Italia, was suitably incoherent as an advertising slogan more than a party name because people could read very different messages into its meaning, most importantly, the "new and improved" designation associated with the products Berlusconi advertised on his TV channels and the cross-class and cross-geographical attraction of linking the party to one of the few widely accepted symbols of Italian national unity: the national soccer team. Even as late as November 1993, however, Berlusconi still refused to commit himself publicly to the new party he was already organizing from within his business.

Once he had maneuvered himself into a position where his entry into politics seemed all but inevitable, by removing potential challenges such as that from Indro Montanelli, the conservative but independent editor of the Berlusconi-owned newspaper *Il Giornale*, and by having the leading politicians of the day, Achille Ochetto of the PDS and Gianfranco Fini of the newly named AN, as commentators following the public announcement of his arrival on the political scene on a video transmitted on his three networks on January 29, 1994, Berlusconi moved into high gear. If Berlusconi's Fininvest served as the nerve center for the establishment of Forza Italia, with the company's executives and staff throughout Italy as its main agents, Berlusconi himself was more concerned with crafting a message for the center-right as whole, laying out an election strategy based on marketing himself as Italy's savior from regular politicians and recruiting political allies to his side. These tasks were intertwined; and this is where there is some genius to Berlusconi's intervention. He made himself available as a powerful resource for other center-right parties. Partly through appealing to overarching themes such as anti-Communism and the identities of those left stranded politically by *Tangentopoli* and also through shrewdly differentiated appeals to diverse geographical constituencies, Berlusconi was able to craft a center-right coalition based on the fact that his two major potential allies, the Northern League in the North and the National Alliance in the South, had totally different geographical constituencies and thus could enter into coalition with Berlusconi without fear of self-sacrifice. Indeed, it would be Berlusconi who could guarantee them both significant representation in their respective regions of provenance at the potential expense of his party and draw them into an alliance of mutual advantage even if the allies in question had rather different ideological repertoires. What they had in common was this: they were political outsiders largely untainted by *Tangentopoli* but facing years in the political wilderness without access to some broader center-right coalition. They shared the view that victory for the center-left would be bad news for the constituencies they represented, be they government employees or small businesses. In the context of the new electoral system, Berlusconi convinced them that there was no alternative to alliance with him.

With Forza Italia as the middle party, Berlusconi fought the 1994 election with two separate alliances: the Freedom Pole with the League in the North and Center and the Pole of Good Government (with the AN and the neo-Christian Democrat CCD) in much of the South. The critical electoral issue was the need to have single candidates for the coalition in each single-member seat (475 deputies and 230 senators). A related, if secondary, problem was how to represent the component parties of the coalition in the multi-member districts (155 seats in the Chamber and eighty-three in the Senate). In each case, sacrifices for the whole would have to be made by the parts, complicated by the geographical distribution of secure and marginal seats (as suggested by prior elections) and strong and weak candidates (relative to both party organization and local roots). If on the left (the "Progressives") PDS provided a relatively stable pole around which to organize a coalition, the center-right seemed in an even more difficult position in an electoral sense. But because the decision of "no enemy on the left" brought the radical left into prominence within the center-left, the centrist elements drifted away from it and there was much dispute over the program, who would be prime minister in the event of victory, and whether parties would actually enter into a government (Di Virgilio 1994, 504–11). On the center-right, the League was violently opposed to any direct alliance with AN, however "post-Fascist" it now claimed to be; but Berlusconi, closed off from a centrist option by his failure to strike deals with either Segni or Martinazzoli, successfully and rapidly negotiated two pacts between officially entering into national politics on January 26 and February 11, 1994: one with the League and various minor parties in the North and Center and one with AN and various minor parties in the South. For the election to the Chamber of Deputies this produced five different geographical candidacy patterns, although two were dominant (Figure 4.1). In the North and Center, except in Umbria and the Marche, FI ran with the League as the Freedom Pole, whereas in much of the South (and the islands) FI ran with the AN as the Pole of Good Government. In the Marche, FI and AN ran separate candidates. In some districts, the FI and CCD ran against AN, and in two provinces in the South FI and AN ran against the CCD. A somewhat different pattern prevailed for the Senate election. The relative weakness of FI in the peninsula South and the enmities between AN and the CCD (particularly in Abruzzo and Campania) account for much of this geographical variance. All together, however, the pattern of candidacies on the center-right suggests both how difficult it was for Berlusconi (unlike the left and the center) to put together a *national* coalition and how much the process was driven by electoral rather than by ideological or programmatic considerations.[6] It reinforces the view that the creation of the center-right was at base a geographical operation, appealing to distinct constituencies in different places by offering them distinctive menus of electoral choice.

Berlusconi was the national "glue" to the center-right electoral setup. It was his TV channels and the consequent ability to disseminate his relentlessly optimistic message of a businessman bringing his demonstrated capacity to solve problems to government that wove together new recruits to FI from the old parties with the established voters of the League and AN. At the same time Berlusconi appealed to all those threatened by center-left government activism he also eased the negative image of the outsider parties beyond their core constituencies by bringing them into his alliance. His wild promises, such as the claim that he would create "a million new jobs," contrasted with the fairly conservative program of austerity measures and fiscal rectitude, given the serious problems of the Italian economy, proposed by the center-left. Organized by Berlusconi through Fininvest, the election campaign made extensive use of polling techniques imported from presidential campaigns in the United States to both test out slogans and proposals and to use the resulting data to advertise his popularity (see, e.g., Pagnoncelli 2001).

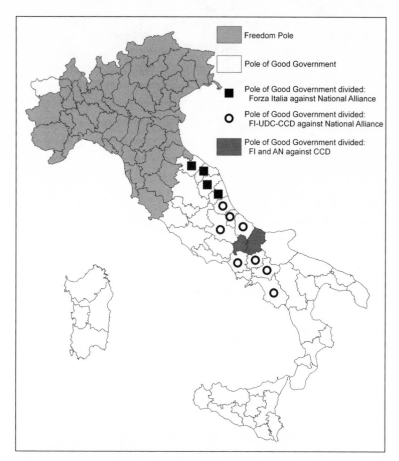

Figure 4.1   The geography of center-right electoral offerings, Italian Chamber of Deputies, 1994.

Anti-Communism, Berlusconi as a "new" force in politics, and opposition to the "old parties" were the overarching themes of the campaign. Though potentially unifying across both alliances, with the first theme particularly attractive to AN and the third especially popular with the League, the emphasis on the "leader" also raised difficulties, particularly within the League with its own authoritarian leadership. Be that as it may, almost immediately after declaring his involvement, polls began to report the net superiority of the

TABLE 4.1   VOTE SHARE AND SEAT ALLOCATIONS FOR THE
TWIN ALLIANCES IN THE CHAMBER OF DEPUTIES AND SENATE,
1994 ELECTIONS.

	Chamber of Deputies, % of vote	Chamber of Deputies, % of seats	Senate, % of vote	Senate, % of seats
Poles of Freedom and Good Government	42.9	58.1	40.4	49.2
Progressives	34.4	33.8	33.2	38.8
Other	22.7	8.1	26.4	12.0
Total	100	100	100	100

elements of the two alliances relative to the left and center groups (Sani 1994, 425). This was to hold up through the March election. The consensus view is that Berlusconi's control over his own television channels and ability to attract the attention of the state-owned ones contributed significantly to the rapid ascent of FI as an electoral force. Certainly, careful empirical studies suggest that Berlusconi and FI had the lion's share of media attention. Even the putatively left-wing RAI 3 gave more time to FI in particular and the right-wing alliances in general than to the left or to the center (Segatti 1994, 486). But this indicates that the capacity to ensure *exposure* of his message more than *control* over channels was the secret to Berlusconi's media success. In Italy as a whole, the outcome of the 1994 election was mainly positive for the twin alliances on the center-right (see Table 4.1). In the Chamber they had a majority but in the Senate they fell three seats shy of victory. But the message had fallen on the most fertile ground only in some places (Diamanti and Mannheimer 1994). The two center-right coalitions won the majority of single-member seats in northern Italy, Sicily, and in a scattering of provinces in the peninsula South (above all in Lazio, Campania, and Puglia) (see Figure 4.2). The demographic weight of Lombardy, Lazio, Campania, Puglia, and Sicily was particularly telling in the outcome as it would be in any Italian national election. In the South as a whole, however, the victories were by much smaller margins than those in the North (Bartolini and D'Alimonte 1994, 652). In the proportional contests, FI did best in the North

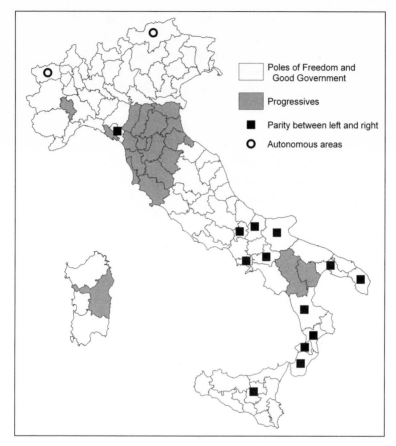

Figure 4.2   The geography of political majorities, 1994 elections.

and in Sicily, with the League sharing the northern limelight and AN doing well in parts of the South (Ricolfi 1994, 604). Central Italy and the "inner" peninsula South proved largely immune to either Berlusconi's siren song or his allies in both components of the election.

Though Berlusconi was the leader of both coalitions, it is impossible to determine from the outcome of the majoritarian contests how important he and Forza Italia were to the overall results of the election. To do this we need to look to the results of the proportional part of the election to determine what the overall impact was. Keeping in mind the discussion in Chapter 3 of how parties replace one another geographically in their relative levels of support, we can distinguish among a number of ways in which Forza Italia could have operated in inserting itself into the electoral system relative to both its putative potential constituency (particularly former DC and PSI voters) and its electoral allies (AN and the League). Recalling the measures of spatial clustering described in Chapter 3, it is of particular interest to see how much the clustering of support for FI in 1994 (and subsequently in the proportional components of the 1996 and 2001 elections) fails to parallel that of DC in 1992, the last time that party appeared on the ballot (see Figure 4.3). Historically, high levels of support for DC had been concentrated in the Northeast and in parts of the South (see Chapter 3). However, by 1992, DC and the PSI had effectively "southernized" (see Figure 4.3, top left-hand panel). Interestingly, and strongly suggestive of FI's mobilization of a distinctly "new" electorate, in 1994 FI votes clustered strongly in the Northwest. In the peninsula South support was heavily clustered in a few areas, with low support in the surrounding districts.[7] Only in Sicily did FI directly replace DC. By 1996 and 2001 FI did achieve stronger clusters of support in the peninsula South, suggesting that Berlusconi's message (and organization) took some time to attain a breakthrough there. The greatest clustering of support, however, remained the Northwest and Sicily.

The "middle party" view of FI, as not so much the heir to DC but as continuing and revolutionizing Craxi's appeal to particularistic voters attracted by the image of the leader and the prospect of personal benefits, is supported not only by the spatial analysis but also by polling data suggesting that voting for FI in 1994 was an "anti-ideological" vote drawing support from voters across the previous political spectrum (including the left) but particularly those in places occupied with problems (crime, economic development, personal insecurity) to which the "ideological" parties (PDS, AN, etc.) had no solution other than Roman business-as-usual. Ricolfi (1994) refers to this in terms of the "secularization" of political appeals and the net movement of Italian politics away from the "church-parties"

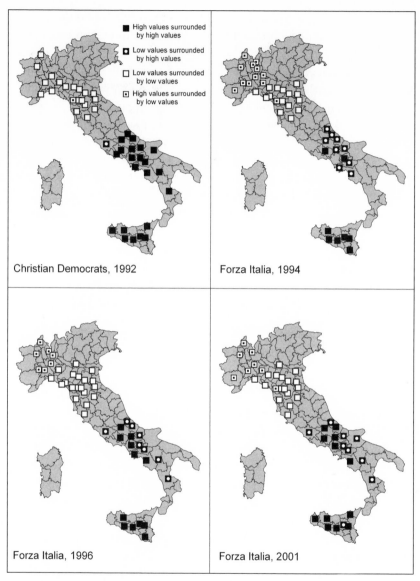

Figure 4.3 Geographic clustering of support for the Christian Democrats (1992) and Forza Italia (1994, 1996, 2001).

(DC and the PCI) that had dominated before 1992. In this perspective, FI represented an innovative force more in tune with the outlook of a large portion of the electorate, at least in the most secularized places, than did the other parties on right, center, or left. Among other things it represented a decisive shift away from rather than a simple replacement of DC at the epicenter of Italian electoral politics.[8]

The other main parties in Berlusconi's coalition, the AN and the League, provided rather more continuity in 1994 between the old party system and the new one than did Forza Italia. Aligned with Berlusconi's center-right FI, the AN has consistently outperformed its predecessor in each election since 1992. In this respect, the AN not only inherited the majority of MSI support, but it also appears to have mobilized new voters and former supporters of the disappeared DC and the PSI in these places (Agnew, 1997). Figure 4.4 portrays how the AN replaced the MSI geographically. The 1992 panel (upper left) serves as a benchmark and maps significant local Moran's I values for the MSI the last time that it appeared on the ballot. Statistically significant regional clusters of high support (solid black squares) are present around Rome and in the Puglia region (the heel of Italy), while a large cluster of low support (white squares) fans out across northern Italy. In northwest Italy there are a few spatial outliers, or provinces, that contain high support for the MSI, but these are surrounded by provinces with low MSI support (i.e., small black squares within larger white squares). Prior to comparing the 1992 map to the 1994, 1996, and 2001 maps, it is important to recall that the bivariate form of the local Moran's I index is invoked for the next three panels in Figure 4.4 and thus requires a slightly different interpretation.

Regional clusters of high support around Rome and in Puglia (solid black squares) indicate that high levels of support for the AN in 1994, 1996, and 2001 are surrounded by similarly high levels of 1992 MSI support, thus suggesting a degree of spatiotemporal stability between the old MSI and new AN. The cluster of white squares in northern Italy denotes low levels of AN support in 1994, 1996, and 2001 are surrounded by similarly low levels of 1992 MSI

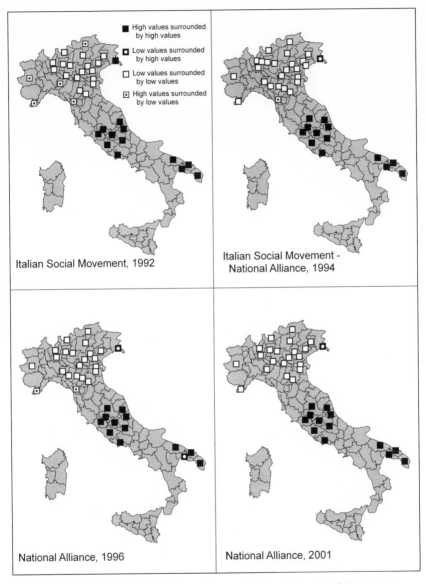

Figure 4.4 Geographic clustering of support for the Italian Social Movement (1992) and National Alliance (1994, 1996, 2001).

support, suggesting that much of the North (except Trieste) remains unreceptive to the post-Fascist Italian right, despite its efforts to broaden its appeal. There are relatively few spatial outliers, or provinces with high AN support surrounded by low 1992 MSI support (i.e., small black squares within white squares) or conversely, low AN support surrounded by high 1992 MSI support (i.e., small white circles surrounded by black squares). Overall, the continuity of clustering of MSI and AN support between 1992 and 2001, and the relative lack of new spatial outliers, illustrates how in this case replacement may be analogous to substitution without any colonization or much mobilization.

In 1994 FI and the League were in the position of having to "share" northern Italy, with the League having much its best showing in the Northeast. Overall, however, the League had a disappointing election compared to both 1992 (from 8.7 to 8.4 percent) and to polling numbers collected prior to Berlusconi's announcement of the formation of FI in January 1994 (as high as 21 percent in October 1993 but down to 11 percent by early February 1994) (Ricolfi 1994, 590). Very quickly, therefore, FI began to steal much of the League's electoral thunder. How it did so needs explanation. Located in northeastern Italy, the Veneto was one of the historic strongholds for DC, and is one of the regions where the League initially found its greatest support (see Chapter 3). Although no significant amounts of spatiotemporal clustering are visible in the northeast of Italy for DC in 1992 and FI in 1994 in Figure 4.3, initial levels of League support more or less mirrored that of the former DC, and it is often presumed that the League substituted for the DC in the Veneto and in some other parts of northern Italy on a more-or-less one-for-one basis (e.g., Diamanti 2003a; Golden 2004). And although divisions within the party and its base later marginalized what was for a while the largest party in northern Italy, the alliance with Berlusconi's FI beginning in 1994 was largely on the League's terms. In the Veneto, for example, the League received twenty-two out of the thirty-six majoritarian seats won by the Pole of Feedom because Berlusconi had given the League's candidates a free run in this component of the election, although its share of the proportional vote in the region was fully two percent points less than that of FI (21.6 percent compared to 23.6) (Riccamboni 1994, 119).[9]

Using election data from the 582 municipalities of the Veneto, Table 4.2 reports provincial estimates of voter transitions from the DC in 1992 to the League and FI in 1994, 1996, and 2001, or in other words, the proportion of voters who supported the DC in 1992 and who also voted for the League or FI in 1994, 1996, or 2001. Note that 1992 is used as the baseline year for comparison because it is the last year the DC appeared on the ballot and we are specifically interested in how the DC was replaced in the region by the League and FI. Voter transitions from the DC to FI and the Northern League in the Veneto are estimated using King's (1997; 2002) method of ecological inference. Other methods, such as entropy maximization, could be used to estimate such transitions, but King's method has a relatively low threshold in terms of data requirements and was used previously to examine national-level voter transitions in consecutive elections in Italy (Benoit et al. 2004; Wellhofer 2001) but not party replacement per se. Based upon constrained maximum likelihood analysis, party replacement estimates are obtained from the identity $T_i = \beta_i^b X_i + \beta_i^w (1 - X)$ where the independent variable, X, is the vote share for the old party in the first or baseline election, and the dependent variable, T, is the vote share for the new party in a subsequent election. The quantity of particular interest is β_i^b, the percentage of voters who supported the old party in the baseline election and who also voted for the new party in a subsequent election.

Several interesting features emerge from the table of voter transitions. First, the regional transition estimates mask notable provincial (i.e., subregional) differences. For example, at the regional level it is estimated that 28 percent of former-DC voters voted for the League in 1994. In the province of Rovigo, however, the estimate is only 13 percent, but in Venice and Verona the estimate approaches 40 percent. Second, there are notable variations in the estimates over time. In most provinces, both the League and FI receive moderate levels of support from former-DC voters in 1994, in 1996 it appears that former-DC voters tended to favor the League (when it ran alone), but in 2001 there was a reversal of electoral fortunes with

TABLE 4.2. PARTY REPLACEMENT ESTIMATES FOR THE
DC TO LN/FI IN THE VENETO, 1992–2001.

	Voter transitions from the DC, 1992					
	LN94	LN96	LN01	FI94	FI96	FI01
Belluno	0.37	0.57	0.12	0.18	0.28	0.31
Padova	0.33	0.52	0.18	0.29	0.19	0.47
Rovigo	0.13	0.32	0.11	0.24	0.22	0.35
Treviso	0.32	0.57	0.21	0.28	0.18	0.51
Venezia	0.37	0.66	0.19	0.28	0.14	0.46
Verona	0.38	0.64	0.27	0.05	0.05	0.26
Vicenza	0.22	0.47	0.30	0.25	0.14	0.51
Veneto	0.28	0.41	0.21	0.22	0.11	0.47

former-DC voters supporting FI over the League. Closer inspection
reveals some notable transitions, such as that from the DC to FI in
Verona. In 1994 and 1996 it is estimated that only some 5 percent of
former DC supporters voted for Berlusconi's party in that province,
but by 2001 this figure was 26 percent. Such a dramatic increase is
consistent with the argument that in the Veneto FI was slowly colonizing former-DC space *and* effectively mobilizing new voters.

The geographical instability and temporal volatility of voter
transition estimates in Table 4.2 illustrates clearly that the process of
party replacement and electoral change across the Veneto was far
more complex than the simple and direct substitution of the DC
with the Northern League. Therefore, in this regard, the 1994 result
perhaps understated the degree to which Berlusconi had made inroads into the region (and possibly elsewhere in the Northeast) but
mainly and, later, increasingly as a substitute for the League. In particular, for those business sectors more interested in governmental
reform than perpetual protest, Forza Italia brought respite from the
political instability of the region since the erosion of DC. As noted
by Ilvo Diamanti at the time (1994, 56): "If the League was 'the revolt,' Berlusconi represented for the voters the 'quiet after the revolt:' the possibility of reconciling with the past, closing the books
on the tensions of the present." If before the election of 1994, the
League thought it had bested Berlusconi, these data suggest that this
was already a problematic notion and, in the end and at the national

level, as previously established, it was AN that held up better as independent force in the coalition in the face of Berlusconi and his seemingly "instant" middle party. This dilemma for the League was not going to be easy to resolve. "For the League, the ally chosen to win the election became the true antagonist" (Diamanti 1994, 56). Notwithstanding these auguries, Italy had entered the age of Berlusconi.

The new Berlusconi government at once set about dealing with its main priorities: keeping the new prime minister out of legal trouble and trying to keep its various parties and their supporters happy (Stille 2006, 180–204). The latter involved, for example, plans for tax and illegal building amnesties and various proposals for gargantuan public works. Little or no effort was directed toward reforming the public sector or stimulating a more transparent national economy. Such neoliberal policies would have brought too many of the government's supporters into open rebellion. The former priority was to prove more problematic politically, however. In July 1994, in the face of the imminent arrest of Berlusconi's brother under the charge of bribing tax inspectors, the government decreed that the judicial authorities could no longer issue arrest warrants for a set of crimes, including financial fraud and corruption. Crucially, all of the defendants still in detention for corruption were released. Immediately, the main Milan prosecutors announced their resignations with their most famous member, Antonio Di Pietro, publicly berating the government. Berlusconi's main allies, the League and AN, were swift in their denunciations of the decree. Media frenzy on Berlusconi's behalf failed to prevent a disastrous ebb in his popular support. Those who live by the polls die by them. Subsequent corruption charges against Fininvest executives and then Berlusconi's own indictment in November 1994 undermined whatever else the government intended to do. At the same time, Umberto Bossi had concluded that this government was neither good for his movement's future electoral prospects nor likely to achieve any of the goals that he sought, particularly devolution of governmental powers to the northern regions. Beginning in July 1994 Bossi increasingly distanced himself from Berlusconi and, finally, in mid-December made a formal break with the government. Berlusconi tried to convince many of the League's parliamentarians to remain allied with Forza Italia but this was ultimately to no avail. The government collapsed amid much acrimony after a brief seven and a half months. However, rejoicing on the center-left was to prove injudicious. Berlusconi would be back.

But it would not be in 1996. The League stood alone in that year's national election and in so doing deprived Berlusconi of a likely victory. Apart from the retrenchment of the League's vote in its northern heartland, nothing much changed from 1994 (see Figure 4.5). The League received 10.8 percent of the national vote for the Chamber in the majoritarian component and 10.1 in the proportional; enough to deny the FI-AN alliance a victory even though with the League the center-right would have had a 51.1 to 45.3 percent advantage in the former and 52.2 to 43.3 percent advantage in the latter. Following the 1996 election, the League refocused its energies away from "Roman politics" toward its symbolic campaign of achieving independence for "Padania" or a large tract of northern Italy. Electorally, this proved to be something of a wild goose chase. The "chameleon" quality of the League as a political actor, already noted in 1994 (Pajetta 1994), came back to haunt it. Bossi slowly abandoned any claim to representing a neoliberal approach to economic policy. Those figures in the League most associated with such an approach either left or were expelled. Caught between the desire of at least part of its base to achieve concrete results and the leader's whimsical pursuit of an invented "Celtic" past for his invented region, the party went into an electoral free fall in the late 1990s. In the 1999 European election its vote was less than half that of its 1996 national election total.

Meanwhile, the efforts of AN to pursue an independent course without Berlusconi also foundered. AN's leader, Gianfranco Fini, wished to model the party after the American Republicans or the British Conservative Party, by moving farther away from the party's Fascist roots. But this proved difficult. It remained a regionally based party without much ability to expand elsewhere (see above, Figure 4.4). Initiatives to give it a higher profile failed to deliver. In

Figure 4.5   Geographic distribution of support for the Northern League, 1994–2001. Legend applies to each map in this figure. Provincial percentages in proportional contexts.

particular, its sponsorship of a constitutional referendum strengthening the majoritarian element in the electoral system failed in 1999 as did its alliance with the centrist Mario Segni in the 1999 European elections. As AN and the League were facing their difficulties, Forza Italia went from strength to strength as the main opposition party. In the 1999 European election, it acquired the position as the party with the largest single share of votes (25 percent). The effect of the years in opposition was clear: AN and the League needed Berlusconi to achieve national influence and office but Berlusconi needed them (and the CCD/UDC) if he were to gain a majority of seats in parliament. Forza Italia would never be enough on its own.

In 1996 a relatively more unified center-left than that of 1994 won the national election. As we have argued, this was mainly because of the defection of the League from Berlusconi's camp rather the expansion of the vote for the center-left. But there was some sign of a more integrated political opponent to Berlusconi in that this time there was a candidate for prime minister, the centrist former DC member, Romano Prodi, who began the task of making the center-left more attractive to centrists, and a more compact coalition without the far left. The overall failure of the center-left to make much of Berlusconi's conflicts of interest and judicial difficulties during the election campaign and, indeed, subsequent attempts at bargaining with him over constitutional issues by Massimo D'Alema, leader of the PDS without extracting any concessions on his massive conflicts of interest, made for a weak opponent.[10]

More particularly, and with respect to electoral performance, a number of problems continued to wrack the center-left throughout the 1990s. One problem had to do with the cultural changes of the previous twenty years, such as greater popular egoism and materialism and lessened social solidarity at group and national levels (which Berlusconi so readily exploited). These factors disadvantaged the left, which continued to operate with themes and discourse, such as anti-Fascism and collective identities such as "workers" or the "poor," that reflected the left's ideological core: its historic hostility to social inequality (Anderson 2002; Cartocci 2002; Perna 2006). Another problem was the decline of parties as direct political mediators with the rise of coalitions. Although this was a problem across the board, it was particularly problematic on the center-left because of the difficulty of bringing together under one rubric the left of DC and secular groups (such as the Radicals) in the face of probable political dominance by the heirs of the PCI (Biorcio 1994). Such old ideological rivals could not be readily combined. Only after attempts at going it alone in the center failed in 1994 did the left of DC slowly make its way into a redefined center-left (Augias and Covotta 2005). Yet, this still left unresolved the question of how to mediate between Catholic and lay sensibilities (Diamanti and Ceccarini 2007).

However, in terms of achieving national success, perhaps the main weight of the heritage of the left has been its geographical concentration in central Italy and its long-standing inability to penetrate well into the population centers of the North. As the PCI split up in the early 1990s, its main heirs, the PDS and Refounded Communists, remained largely parties of central Italy (see Figure 4.6). The red belt of the PCI is clearly visible as a patch of solid black squares in the middle of the Italian peninsula, where high levels of support for the PCI are significantly clustered (upper-left panel). The lone spatial outlier of low PCI support surrounded by high PCI support (i.e., small white circle within a black square) in the red zone is the province of Lucca. Due in part to long-standing legacies of small-scale landownership, and Lucca's historical status as an independent republic, the Italian left has always had difficulties

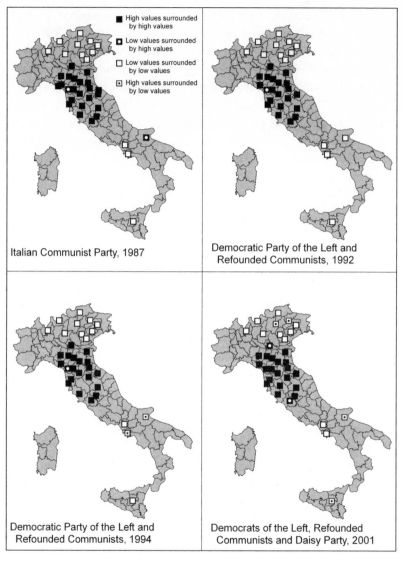

Figure 4.6. Geographic clustering of support for the Italian Communist Party (1987) and the new parties of the left (1994, 1996, 2001).

garnering support in this province (Agnew 2002, Chapter 6). With the advent of the Margherita Party (led mainly by former left-DC figures) even Lucca has moved into the center-left column (bottom-right panel). A significant cluster of low PCI support is also visible in the northeast of Italy, and coincides with an area referred to as the 'white zone' where the Christian Democrats (DC) fared particularly well in the immediate post–World War II period.

The remaining bivariate LISA maps explore the relationship between aggregated support for the PDS and RC in 1992 and 1994, aggregated support for the DS, RC, and center-left Margherita (former DC) Party in 2001, and 1987 PCI support (results for 1996 are omitted due to space limitations). The purpose of aggregating support for parties of the new Italian left is to illustrate party replacement as the splitting of old PCI votes. Note that between 1996 and 2001, the PDS renamed itself the Democrats of the Left (DS), the RC splintered into two parties and that the Margherita (Daisy) Party emerged as a promising option for many voters on the center-left of the Italian political spectrum. Notwithstanding such name changes, party splits, and new additions to the Italian left, the map sequence in Figure 4.6 is remarkably consistent. High levels of support for the parties of the left, namely the PDS and RC in 1992 and 1994, and the DC, RC, and Margherita in 2001 are surrounded by similarly high 1987 PCI values in central Italy. The Northeast remains an area of low support for the Italian left in spatiotemporal terms, though two significant spatial outliers of high support surrounded by low support emerge in 2001. The stability of most of the clusters in Figure 4.6 is expected, but the two outliers in northeast Italy may indicate that the new Italian left is making inroads into what was once a DC stronghold, as well as elsewhere (e.g., Puglia).

Finally, outside of the traditional red belt of central Italy, and islands of support elsewhere, particularly in the inner peninsula South, the center-left has lost its connection with the general populace of salaried employees. It appeals more to certain sectors of the middle class, such as teachers, than to those traditionally associated with "labor" politics such as factory workers. Indeed, even within its historic strongholds there was to be strong evidence of erosion of its vote and inroads by the center-right, for example, in the high percentage of votes (above the national average) given by red-belt housewives (the quintessential television-watching Berlusconi voters) to Forza Italia in 2001 (Ramella 2005, 200).

Rebuilding the Center-Right, 2000–2001

If 1994 proved to be a false start in making Berlusconi's Italy (and vice versa), the prospective election of 2001 looked much more favorable because of the exhaustion of a series of center-left governments that had imposed a degree of fiscal restraint on Italy (mainly in anticipation of joining the new currency, the euro, in 1999) and that were always on the verge of collapse because of policy and personality differences between the component parties (particularly between the two leaders, Prodi and D'Alema). Berlusconi also had new leverage over his potential partners that he could now hope to exercise given their weakened state. Berlusconi had three major advantages over his adversaries going into the May 2001 national election. The first advantage was that in the absence of Prodi, now president of the European Commission in Brussels (who had clear centrist credentials), Berlusconi could return to his favorite theme of anti-Communism in relation to his putative opponents, even though Francesco Rutelli of the Margherita Party became the center-left candidate for prime minister.

This time around, Berlusconi could also personalize the campaign more than before by making his face not only the symbol on every Forza Italia poster but by featuring his life story (through the free distribution of a lavishly illustrated book about him to twelve million households, *Una Storia Italiana*) as a key element of his campaign narrative about the gospel of individual success and the optimistic story—stolen again from the U.S. Republicans—of an "economic dawn" for Italy if only Berlusconi were in charge. He also shamelessly expropriated the idea of Newt Gingrich's (1994) "Contract with America" to lay out five "promises" of a "Contract with Italians" that, in true populist style, was between *him* and the people, not between either his party or the center-right coalition and the population.[11] This was possible now because Forza Italia was clearly the dominant partner on the center-right, not simply the "glue" between two separate alliances. In 2001 Forza Italia, the League, AN, and the CCD/UDC were to run as a single alliance with Berlusconi as the supreme leader. Finally, his use of the media to disseminate misleading (and false) polling numbers created a series of expectations about the outcome of the election designed to discourage the less mobilized of center-left voters. This is where Berlusconi's control over the three major private TV channels proved more crucial than his putative use of them to convert anyone to his cause. As a result, the main theme of the media (including the non-Berlusconi press and TV) became not whether Berlusconi would win but, rather, by how much.

Much attention has been given to the personalized nature of the 2001 election campaign, with Berlusconi and Rutelli center-stage as explicit candidates for "prime minister," Berlusconi's capacity to use the media to his advantage, and the deficiencies of the center-left, primarily the way that the Refounded Communists, in rejecting entry into the center-left Olive Tree coalition, siphoned off a critical 5 percent of the vote in the proportional component. Commented on less often but more crucial, in our estimation, was the relative political integration of the center-right coalition and, more particularly, its geographical scope. Berlusconi certainly "mattered," but he did not matter in the way usually ascribed to him. According to polls, his image had only a fairly limited impact on the vote. Other leaders had similar or higher ratings (ITANES 2001, 125–42). More important had been his investment in the FI machine (which was well prepared for the election), the binding agreements he made with his coalition partners, his selection of the central themes of the election to which his partners conformed, and his imposition of a "brand" identity on the center-right as a whole (Diamanti and Lello 2005, 21). As a result of Berlusconi's efforts, the center-right coalition seemed to have a coherence in the eyes of its voters that the center-left seemed to be lacking, insofar as survey results are a guide (ITANES 2001, 144–45). Decisive to this impression, given the negative outcome in 1996 without its presence in the coalition, was successfully bringing the League back into the fold. After the League's electoral debacles in the late 1990s, the provocative strategy of northern secessionism seemed to have led nowhere. According to one account, by the right-wing journalist Feltri (2006), as early as 1997 Bossi was already thinking of changing his political direction. However, whether this would have included a return to Berlusconi's side at that time seems doubtful, given the persisting rancor. Finally, in 2000 Bossi and Berlusconi did make up with one another by agreeing to jointly pursue a policy of "devolution" (the new word of Bossi's first used in 1999 concerning decentralization of governmental powers, but now pertaining to the regions and provinces rather than to the North as a whole).[12] This signaled both Berlusconi's almost desperate desire to have the League in his coalition for obvious electoral reasons and his willingness to potentially alienate his other allies in doing so. In his eyes, attending to the North was fundamental to victory by the center-right. But it also represented a turnabout by the League toward acceptance of the fact that achieving their ideas of a more empowered northern Italy to any extent (while hanging on to whichever voters they had left) required settling with Berlusconi once and for all. To seal the deal and reassure voters that there would be no repeat of 1994, Bossi and Berlusconi signed an agreement that in return for concurring that the coalition would pursue devolution, guaranteed that the League would give its support to the rest of Berlusconi's program. This was to produce a privileged "northern axis" within the post-2001 government and perpetual trouble between the League, on the one hand, and the AN and the UDC which Bossi tagged as "professional politicians" of the old school plotting for a future without Berlusconi, on the other, that Berlusconi was to spend considerable political energy mediating (Albertazzi and McDonnell 2005, 956).

Berlusconi had been at work preparing for his return since the fall of the Prodi government on October 9, 1998. It proved effective. The overall result was positive for the center-right but with little or no change in the geographical structure of the vote from 1996 save for the reintegration of (a much reduced) vote from the League into the Berlusconi column. The biggest difference was in the absolute centrality of Forza Italia to the coalition's overall results. In 2001 FI received far and away the largest share of the total vote of any single party (in the proportional part of the Chamber election) (29.4 percent compared to 20.6 percent in 1996) and, indicating its new role as a putative national party, it finished first in eighty-one out of 101 provinces. Indeed, it was first everywhere except in the strongholds of the left, mainly in central Italy. Even there, it generally finished second. With 60 percent of the center-right vote (relative to 40 percent in 1994), FI was now very much the senior partner in the coalition. AN polled considerably less than it had in 1994 and 1996, the CCD/UDC saw a serious loss of votes (mainly to FI), and the League vote collapsed (again largely to the benefit of FI) gaining less than half (4 percent) what it had obtained in 1996. The centrality of FI translated into an image of greater coherence for the center-right as a whole. Even though party loyalties remained relatively stronger on the right than on the left, this produced a particularly important premium for the center-right among voters in the majoritarian component of the election (total center-right 45.4 compared to 43.2 for the center-left) and, as a result, a much larger parliamentary majority than it had enjoyed in 1994 (Berselli and Cartocci 2001).

If "Berlusconi ate his allies" (Berselli and Cartocci 2001, 453), he still had needed their votes to win. In return, the placement of their candidates in "safe" majoritarian seats had presciently given them enhanced representation over what their actual votes would have deserved. However, the basis for new discipline within the coalition was that they now owed Berlusconi, not the other way around. What had come to pass? In the majoritarian component nothing overwhelming changed from 1994 (Figure 4.7, compare Figure 4.2). If anything, the main shift since 1994 was an erosion of the center-right coalition vote in Liguria, Piedmont, and the Veneto to the benefit of the center-left, a consolidation of the center-right in Sicily, and a complex pattern of localized expansion and contraction of the coalition in the peninsula South (e.g., expansion in Abruzzi and Lazio; contraction in Campania and Calabria). Moreover, if in the North the center-left now often crept in by small majorities, in the South many of the marginal districts were captured

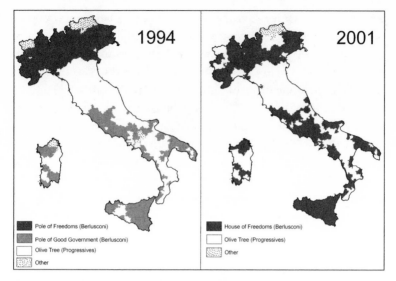

Figure 4.7   Electoral geography of majoritarian vote, 1994 and 2001.

by the center-right in 2001. Given the greater overall volatility of southern voters and the greater number of marginal seats in the South as whole, this made the center-right potentially more of a hostage to fortune in the majoritarian component of the electoral system than it did the center-left.

In the proportional component, the story in 2001 was very different from 1994 (or 1996). This time, FI ate directly into the electorates of its allies. It did so at the expense of the League in the Northeast (see above, Table 4.2) and of AN and CCD/UDC in the South. In the North this was not anything new, as argued previously, but in the South this was a novelty. Though AN remained trapped in its strongholds in the upper South and Puglia (see Figure 4.4), it suffered some erosion of its vote in precisely these areas in 2001 mainly through defections to FI (Diamanti 2001). What is most interesting about the performance of FI in 2001, however, is not so much its expansion at the expense of its coalition allies but its consolidation in areas where it had already acquired something of a base in the national elections of the 1990s. It was not making itself central to the center-right by taking over the places where its allies were strong so much as establishing its own geographical strongholds chiefly where DC and PSI had previously held sway. This led some commentators to see the FI (yet again) as an emergent DC but this is to ignore the totally different appeal of FI (as first noted by Ricolfi 1994) and its continuing association with the right more than the center (Berselli and Cartocci 2001). It certainly did not present itself to the electorate in 2001 as either a confessional or an ideological party of the center. By way of illustration for its geographical grounding, in 2001 Forza Italia gained more than 34 percent of the vote in 120 districts. These districts were concentrated above all in Lombardy, the Veneto, Liguria, Piedmont (in the North), Lazio, Campania, Sardinia, and Sicily (in the South). In sixty-three of these districts FI had previously scored more than 26 percent of the vote in 1994 and 25 percent in 1996. Using these numerical criteria, Diamanti (e.g., 2001, 2003) has identified a "blue zone" or *zona azzurra* in which FI became the dominant political party (see Chapter 2). This stretches from Milan to Cuneo in the Northwest and includes most of Sardinia (Oristano and Cagliari) and the whole of Sicily, save for the province of Enna where it is weaker. FI's success in Lazio and Campania was more vulnerable, and elsewhere its success was relatively fresh in 2001: Verona, Vicenza, and Padua in the Northeast and Como and Sondrio in Lombardy. In these places the growth in FI's vote was at the expense of the League. In Puglia, expansion in 2001 was to the cost of AN.

In this reading, FI is not simply a cyber or media force and Berlusconi is not simply a national candidate with equal appeal everywhere. It was in the "blue zone" (adopting Berlusconi's association of himself and FI with the national soccer team: "the blues") that Berlusconi's message played the best and where a significant segment of the population came to identify with him and his party. As argued in what has proved to be a seminal article, Ricolfi (1994) sees these places as having both histories of secularization, the absence of strong ties to the two great Italian political "churches" of pre-1992, DC, and the PCI, and, of course, their own particularities (Sicily is hardly "the same" socially and economically as, say, Cuneo or Milan) that in different ways open them up for the particularistic and nonideological appeal of Berlusconi. Plausibly, if we take Berlusconi at his word and his supporters as having heard what he said, the overwhelming appeal of FI to its constituencies in those places in the twin axes across the Northwest and across the islands that constituted the blue zone in 2001 was the promise of being left to their own devices except when they might need something from the state (also see Chapter 2).

Conclusion

This chapter has shown how Berlusconi molded a center-right pole in Italian politics between 1994 and 2001. It is hardly a simple linear story. Indeed, after a brief initial success in 1994, Berlusconi had to wait until 2001 to finally reap a political return on his massive investment of economic and political resources. Drawing from his own well-developed connections and the inspiration of Craxi and the PSI in the ancien regime he created his own party from within his business enterprise, Fininvest (later Mediaset), and then set about bringing into the fold of the center-right two political groupings hitherto marginalized within the workings of Italian politics: the Northern League and the National Alliance. This was a difficult task because neither had much in common with the other—ideologically or geographically. In 1994 Berlusconi masterfully created two separate geographical alliances between which he was the political fulcrum: with the League in the North and AN in the South. The 1994 election was a success from his perspective, but his subsequent government quickly collapsed because of both his legal difficulties and the divergent agendas of the League and the other elements in the coalition. In 2001, after a period in which the political fortunes of his allies were in eclipse, he was able to craft a single alliance in which his party, Forza Italia, was finally unquestionably the senior partner. Crucial to his role was Berlusconi's ability to glue together the whole package, using his vast media resources to appeal directly to those people alienated from the state and uninterested in politics yet desirous of a style of life and an ability to control their lives without political hindrance (help was another thing!) that Berlusconi personified but other parties could only either criticize or promise abstractly. So, if Berlusconi's media control was a necessary condition for his political success, it was also an insufficient one. In fact, his own party acquired its own geographical area of electoral strength even as he continued to be the dominant national face of the entire center-right. This suggests not only that the messages of the national media are seen differently in different places but also that party organization and different local contexts continue to play an important role in mediating between national messages, on the one hand, and local responses and likelihoods of voting a certain way on the other.

5

What Went Up Later Came Down

Immediately following the center-right's victory in the 2001 elections, Silvio Berlusconi proclaimed that a "new era" was beginning for all Italians. Indeed, many hopes and expectations were placed upon Berlusconi and his "House of Freedoms" coalition which enjoyed outright majorities in both the Chamber of Deputies and the Senate. Not the least of these expectations was the hope that the Italian economy could be invigorated without damaging the myriad interests of those fearful of the reformist zeal of the center-left. Ushered into power partly because of this appeal, it appeared that Berlusconi could become the strong leader of a stable, long-lasting, and effective government that many Italians had long hoped for. Perhaps more than anyone else, Berlusconi considered himself to be the only leader who could navigate Italy through an ambitious program of tax cuts, devolution, liberalization of services, and pension reform, among other things, that were spelled out during the campaign in his "Contract with Italians" (see Chapters 2 and 4). The programmatic objectives of Berlusconi and the House of Freedoms, however, suffered from circumstances both expected, such as European monetary union and a sluggish economy, and unforeseen, such as the September 11th terrorist attacks and the U.S. preemptive war in Iraq. Similarly, Berlusconi's leadership itself was neither unconditional nor assured as persistent questions about his own conflicts of interest and the cohesiveness of the House of Freedoms were to erode his political clout and tarnish his popularity in the coming years.

As we emphasize in this chapter, internal divisions within Berlusconi's coalition, based largely upon divergent and competing geographical interests, challenged Berlusconi's leadership and his stay in power. This is not to say the center-left Olive Tree coalition would have been immune from similar internal divisions; rather, the success of recent (and past) governments in Italy continues to depend upon the ability to maintain a unified coalition of parties. However, by 2006, the center-right had suffered a series of electoral setbacks in local, regional, and European elections, and the geographical logic of suturing together wildly different policy and personality differences across the coalition partners had begun to disintegrate. As relayed in Chapter 2, this is not that difficult to understand. Increasingly, localized differences in economic development (e.g., Guerrieri and Iammarino 2006) and participatory politics based around hostility to this or that government policy, particularly noticeable in the South (Andrews 2005, Chapters 6 and 7), and an increasingly diversified pattern of patronage politics, some relatively more benign and others more pernicious (Piattoni 1999; 2005), had opened up the political field for a wider range of electoral options in some places and narrowed it elsewhere.[1] This made the center-left potentially more competitive in the South (and, to a lesser extent, in the North) and increased the possibility for electoral poaching across regional boundaries by the various components of the center-right. The glue provided by Forza Italia was drying out, despite Berlusconi's political genius.

On the surface, Berlusconi's second coming in 2001 resembled his initial foray into Italian politics in 1994. In particular, both victories rested upon Berlusconi's ability to form electoral compacts with Umberto Bossi's regionalist Northern League in the North and Gianfranco Fini's post-Fascist National Alliance elsewhere.

However, the lofty expectations for Berlusconi and the House of Freedoms following the 2001 electoral outcome were the result of fundamental differences between his first premiership and his second. First and foremost, and unlike in 1994, the House of Freedoms won a clear majority in 2001 and controlled both houses of Parliament. This certainly allowed Berlusconi a clear shot at carrying out the various programs and reforms that he promised during the election campaign. Second, Berlusconi and his party, Forza Italia, had successfully endured five years in opposition. Given Forza Italia's relatively short history (see Chapter 4), this is a significant accomplishment that served to firmly establish the party and its leader upon the Italian political landscape. Finally, compared to its performance in the 1994 national election, Forza Italia not only broadened its electoral base and appeal across Italy in 2001, but it did so in some places mainly at the expense of its coalition partners. Although Berlusconi and his party did not enjoy an outright majority, Forza Italia was clearly the party around which the House of Freedoms was built in 2001 (see Chapter 4).

Based upon such high expectations, and with the Italian economy buoyed in the short term thanks to the efforts of Berlusconi's predecessor, Romano Prodi, to prepare Italy for entry into the Eurozone, the new government appeared to be well positioned to succeed. Berlusconi's first test emerged when forecasts for Italian economic growth were revised downward shortly after the House of Freedoms took power (Cotta and Verzichelli 2003). Despite a much heralded economic stimulus plan to be put into effect in Berlusconi's first one hundred days, the specter of limited government resources served to highlight fundamental differences between the parties of the center-right coalition, and it brought into focus Berlusconi's role as "coalition-builder" with the seemingly impossible challenge of aligning and reconciling fundamentally competing interests and objectives (Pasquino 2007, 43). For instance, while the Northern League and northern segments of Forza Italia's base clamored for tax cuts and devolution, the National Alliance, UDC (former-centrist CCD and CDU) and southern segments of Forza Italia wanted Berlusconi to make good on his promises of large-scale infrastructure and public works projects. Making matters more difficult for Berlusconi were warnings from the European Union that Italy's budget deficit would likely exceed the previously established 1 percent of GNP target. Caught between campaign promises impossible to keep, a stagnating economy, and the economic constraints of the EU, what Berlusconi needed most was a highly unlikely Italian economic miracle. After describing the broader context and important features of Berlusconi's second government, this chapter examines the electoral-geographic trajectory of Berlusconi's center-right House of Freedoms coalition between 2001 and 2006 that ended with its narrow defeat in 2006.

A Changing Europe, a Stagnant Italy?

As alluded to above, the euphoria surrounding the introduction of the Euro and the new Berlusconi government in 2001 were short-lived. After the dot-com bubble burst on Wall Street, the September 11th terrorist attacks sent the global economy into a tailspin. The following months would bring war to Afghanistan and Iraq, as well as global economic uncertainty. Already resting upon fragile economic fundamentals, such as relying too heavily upon exports, the Italian economy was not in a position to expand, let alone recover. With pressures mounting to adhere to previously agreed upon targets for inclusion within the European monetary zone, it became clear that Berlusconi's ambitious and contradictory program of tax cuts, tax breaks, and increased government spending would be impossible to implement. With little room to maneuver and too few resources to distribute, what once were competing interests within the House of Freedoms would eventually become irreparable cracks and fissures.

Although several circumstances and events would challenge Berlusconi's leadership, issues related to a united Europe proved to be divisive on several levels (Parker 2007). Italy and Italians have long been considered champions of a united Europe, but by virtue, circumstance, and with a little help from the former president of the EU Commission and former prime minister of Italy, Romano

Prodi, the European project became an issue associated with and attributed to the center-left in Italy. As such, Berlusconi and some of the components of the House of Freedoms wanted to distance Italy from "Europe." This separation was first achieved by default when Berlusconi and the House of Freedoms won the 2001 election and became one of the few ruling center-right governments in Europe. Further distancing Berlusconi's Italy from Europe were the economic constraints and targets set by the EU, which in turn called into question whether or not Berlusconi could keep his ambitious campaign promises. Within the House of Freedoms itself, the most vehement and vocal opposition to Europe came from the Northern League. Already pushing for devolution, Italy's commitment and involvement in a (more) united Europe ran directly in the face of the League's anticentralist and radical populist tendencies.

Despite its rather extreme and vocal anti-European stance, Berlusconi tolerated the violent rhetoric and exaggerated theatrics of the Northern League. As noted in Chapter 4, one of the first steps that Berlusconi took to ensure his success and political future before the 2001 election was to create an accord between his party, Forza Italia, and the Northern League. In exchange for the League's unequivocal support on issues and legislation important to Berlusconi, Forza Italia and the prime minister would reciprocate by supporting key items on the League's political agenda, such as federalism/devolution and immigration restrictions. The creation of this "northern axis" between Forza Italia and the League made political sense because the success of the center-right's program hinged upon sustained economic growth. The most likely engine for economic growth in Italy was the North, and it would be the northern regions that would benefit most from the tax cuts and labor market reforms that were specified in Berlusconi's one-hundred-day plan. Given the League's diminished electoral influence within the coalition compared to 1994 (indeed, the League needed Berlusconi far more than he needed the League), the initial cost of this agreement appeared to be minimal to Berlusconi and Forza Italia. As we shall see, however, Berlusconi would pay for this political maneuver that in effect alienated the more southern elements of the House of Freedoms, namely the National Alliance (AN) and Union of Christian Democrats (UDC) (Albertazzi and McDonnell 2005).

As the Berlusconi government became more critical of the requirements for a united Europe, European commentators became more and more skeptical of Berlusconi the leader. One key issue that accentuated this division between Berlusconi's Italy and much of the rest of Europe was the decision to wage a preemptive war on Iraq. As the Bush administration in the United States invented convoluted arguments about Saddam Hussein's links to al-Qaeda, an Iraqi arsenal of weapons of mass destruction, and Iraq's terrorist intentions, opposition to a war in Iraq spread across Europe and in Italy. Despite popular misgivings and majority antiwar sentiment, Berlusconi chose to align himself with Washington over Brussels. The only other major European leader to do so was British Prime Minister Tony Blair. With a more dynamic economy at his disposal, and one that was not constrained by the requirements of the Euro, Prime Minister Blair's margin of error on this foreign policy issue was far greater than that of Berlusconi. The decision to support the war and to send Italian troops to Iraq clearly put Berlusconi on the margins of a Europe united against war and added to existing concerns about his leadership within Italy.

The most persistent questions about Berlusconi's leadership, which actually predate his first term as prime minister in 1994, concerned his numerous conflicts of interest. Frequently formally accused of embezzlement, tax fraud, false accounting, and corruption, Berlusconi faced four separate trials when he entered office in 2001. What made this most remarkable was not the fact that the standing prime minister of one of the largest economies in the world was on trial for much of his term in government, but that his ruling coalition, the House of Freedoms, actually passed legislation that granted him immunity from further prosecution. When challenged about this very issue by a German member of the European Parliament, Martin Schultz, Berlusconi retorted by suggesting that the German MEP audition for a role as "kapo" (a Nazi concentration camp prisoner who was granted privileges in exchange for supervising fellow-prisoners.) in an upcoming film about Nazi concentration camps. Berlusconi's comment was all the more offensive and embarrassing because the Italian government, and more specifically Berlusconi, was presiding over the European Union at the time. Though the immunity law was eventually rejected by the Italian constitutional court, and Berlusconi acquitted of the corruption charge, the impropriety and audacity emanating from Berlusconi and his government further tarnished his credibility and popularity at home and abroad.

Amid the backdrop of war, global economic uncertainty, a struggling domestic economy, and his own legal troubles, it became clear that Berlusconi would not be able to uphold his "Contract with Italians," and his political luster began to fade. Constrained by a small and shrinking tax base and European Central Bank (Eurozone) limits on public spending, Berlusconi and the House of Freedoms became preoccupied with issues of more symbolic than immediately practical importance such as devolution (Diamanti and Lello 2005). With significant differences in opinion existing *within* the center-right coalition on the issue of granting the regions of Italy more economic and political autonomy, the likelihood of any successful legislation related to devolution was always in question (see Chapter 6). Perhaps the most concrete yet still symbolic initiative that Berlusconi championed was the construction of a bridge that would connect Sicily to the mainland. This was precisely the type of large-scale infrastructure and public works project that his southern constituents expected and it had the potential benefit of stimulating the infamously underdeveloped Italian South. More importantly, it would bestow upon Berlusconi the image of a heroic leader who purposefully and successfully helped reunify Italy, the likes of which had not been seen since Giuseppe Garibaldi (or, possibly, Benito Mussolini). Despite concerns about the environmental impact of the bridge, its vulnerability to earthquakes, and the likelihood of the Mafia and other southern interests corrupting the project, a 4.4 billion Euro contract to build the bridge was awarded in 2005. Ultimately, plans for the bridge would be scrapped in 2006 by the new center-left government led by Romano Prodi.

The Beginning of the End?

The House of Freedoms, and in particular Berlusconi and Forza Italia, did not have to wait very long to experience the disapproval of many Italians. In municipal, provincial and regional elections held in the years immediately following the 2001 national election, the House of Freedoms and its constituent parties lost in places where they had consistently won previously and where they were expected to win. In 2002 the center-right lost local elections in Verona, and in 2003 the center-right would lose again in the regional elections of Friuli-Venezia Giulia and in local elections across Sicily. Though subnational elections were not held across Italy, such local contests are frequently used as a diagnostic tool to assess the prevailing political sentiment of the Italian electorate. Despite differences in the nature and logic of local and national elections (Diamanti and Lello 2005), and the difficulties and inconsistencies of projecting local election results onto the national political landscape (Legnante 2004), there is always a high level of interest in both the campaign and results of subnational elections in Italy. For instance, the widespread success of the center-right in the 2000 regional elections ultimately resulted in the resignation of Massimo D'Alema as prime minister and the demise of his center-left government, just as the results of the 2005 regional elections sent the Berlusconi government into crisis. Hence, the local defeats of the House of Freedoms, in some cases in its strongholds, underscored differences within the coalition and the difficulties that the center-right faced when presenting itself and in attracting votes from socially and geographically divergent bases of support.

Italians, and more generally, citizens of European Union member-states, also have the opportunity to vote in elections for European Parliament. Like local elections, these supranational contests can provide valuable insights into the political sentiment of European electorates. As a precursor to future regional and national elections in Italy, the 2004 election for the European Parliament revealed that the Italian center-right, and in particular, Berlusconi and Forza Italia, were losing ground. Recall that in the 2001 national elections,

Berlusconi's Forza Italia finished first in eighty-one of the 101 Italian provinces, and arguably established itself as a national party (see Chapter 4). In a dramatic reversal of electoral fortunes, Forza Italia would finish first in only sixteen provinces in the European election 2004. Moreover, many of the defeats occurred in areas (prematurely) identified as Forza Italia strongholds: the northwest regions of Lombardy, Piedmont, and Liguria, and the southern regions and islands of Sardinia, Sicily, Puglia, and Campania (Diamanti 2003). Making matters worse for Berlusconi were the results from concurrent local elections in which the center-left retook the region of Sardinia, the center-right leaning provinces of Milan, Bergamo, and Padua, and the symbolic "red" city of Bologna.

Although the defeat of Berlusconi's Forza Italia in the 2004 European parliamentary elections was indeed important, perhaps the most significant outcome of the election concerned how it shifted the balance of power within the center-right coalition. Numerically speaking, Berlusconi's party received less than half of the coalitional vote total in the 2004 European election. For comparison, Forza Italia's coalitional vote share was 61 percent in 2001. Of particular interest are where these defeats occurred, which parties benefited, and the implications of these shifts of electoral support. Across the South, Forza Italia's losses were matched by the gains of its coalition partners, the National Alliance, and Union of Christian Democrats (UDC). Similarly, the electoral performance of the Northern League was reinvigorated across many regions of the North. The consolidation of support for Gianfranco Fini's AN and Marco Follini's UDC across the South, primarily at the expense of Forza Italia, galvanized their position relative to Berlusconi's northern axis. Subsequently, Fini threatened to leave the House of Freedoms unless significant changes were made to Berlusconi's economic program, and with the backing of Follini, he demanded the removal of Minister of the Economy, Giulio Tremonti. Recognized to be the guarantor of the northern axis, Tremonti went to great lengths to protect and favor northern interests to the exclusion of southern ones. With ally and League leader, Umberto Bossi, largely absent from the political scene due to illness, and with the balance of power shifting towards the

AN and UDC in the South after the EU elections, Berlusconi ceded to the demands of Fini and Follini. The results from the 2004 EU election illustrate the continued significance of geography to Italian elections, and in particular, the electoral weight of the Italian South.

While the 2004 European election was painful for Forza Italia and Berlusconi's leadership, the returns from the April 2005 regional election proved to be even more problematic. Having lost control of Sardinia and Friuli-Venezia-Giulia in previously held regional elections, the House of Freedoms now lost in twelve of the fourteen regional contests of 2005. Shortly after the center-right's embarrassing regional defeats, deputy prime minister and UDC leader, Marco Follini, demanded that Berlusconi resign, reform his cabinet, and make several policy changes, such as the reduction of taxes for business to help the economic situation in the South. With his demands rejected by Berlusconi, Follini withdrew himself and his party from government on April 15, 2005. Shortly thereafter, the AN's Gianfranco Fini stated that he, too, was considering leaving the government. After emergency talks failed to resolve differences between coalition members, Berlusconi was forced to resign and reassemble a new government with a new platform or face snap elections.

With the support of Italian president Carlo Azeglio Ciampi, Berlusconi avoided elections and created a new cabinet. Basking in the glow of the favorable results from the regional elections, and positioning themselves for the national elections scheduled for 2006, leaders of the center-left chided Berlusconi about there being few if any differences between his previous government, which was the longest-serving government in modern Italian history, and the one formed out of the recent crisis. Indeed, with Follini stepping down as deputy prime minister, Berlusconi brought back his old Forza Italia ally, Giulio Tremonti, to share the post with AN's Gianfrano Fini, who also served as foreign minister. Though Follini's resignation can be viewed as a decision made out of frustration with Berlusconi, it was can also be considered a shrewd political maneuver that served to distance the UDC from Forza Italia in the upcoming national election.

The 2006 Election Campaign, Italian Style

I am the Jesus Christ of politics. I am a patient victim,
I put up with everyone, I sacrifice myself for everyone.

—SILVIO BERLUSCONI
launching his 2006 campaign for reelection.

In the shadow of defeat in the 2005 regional election, the days of
Berlusconi and the House of Freedoms certainly appeared to be
numbered (Campus 2006b). Reinvigorated by its regional victories
and by the return of Romano Prodi from his Brussels sojourn as
President of the EU Commission, the center-left appeared to be
well positioned to perform well in the national election slated for
the spring of 2006. Prior to the establishment of a specific date for
the general election, and in what was considered in Italy and abroad
to be a highly questionable move, discussions about reinstating a
form of the old proportional representation (PR) electoral system
were introduced into Parliament. The proposal for electoral reform
included a majority bonus, or guarantee, of at least 340 seats in the
lower Chamber of Deputies for the winning coalition, and a 4 percent threshold that had to be exceeded in order for a party to be
awarded any seats. Thinly veiled as a necessary reform to reduce the
total number of parties in government, it was clear that the target of
the reform was the center-left coalition, which included several parties that would probably fail to meet the 4 percent threshold. Initial
projections indicated that the reform would indeed enable the House
of Freedoms to remain in power, even if it lost the popular vote (*La
Repubblica* 2005). Despite protests by Prodi and the center-left that
Berlusconi and his allies were changing the rules of the game—as the
game itself was being played—the Berlusconi-controlled government passed the reform.[2]

In addition to improving the coalition's overall chances of remaining in power, the return to PR also afforded the individual parties of the House of Freedoms certain advantages (Newell 2006).
Among the most notable, and perhaps reflecting UDC leader Marco
Follini's post-Berlusconi ambitions, the PR arena would allow the

parties of the center-right to run separately rather than under the umbrella of a coalition, and more precisely, Berlusconi's coalition. This would give voters dissatisfied with Berlusconi and Forza Italia the chance to continue to support the center-right (i.e., AN or UDC) rather than abstaining or voting in protest for the opposition. Given the poor showing of Berlusconi and Forza Italia in previous subnational and European elections, the further the UDC and AN distanced themselves from Berlusconi, the more they stood to benefit at the polls. Additionally, with Berlusconi becoming more a political liability than benefit in recent years, the opportunity for each party to field its own (potential) candidate for prime minister would arguably help to open up yet also confuse the question about who should lead the government.

With few tangible accomplishments after five years in government, Berlusconi and the House of Freedoms kicked off the 2006 election campaign with vaguely familiar promises of tax cuts, increases in pension benefits and economic measures that would stimulate the struggling Italian economy. Offering a succinct platform consisting of easily digestible points, Berlusconi's campaign again relied upon sound bites and the belief that there is no such thing as bad publicity.[3] By contrast, in both substance and style, leader of the center-left Union coalition, Romano Prodi, offered a nearly three-hundred-page election manifesto. Though well respected and recognized across Europe and Italy after having served successfully as president of the European Commission in Brussels, Prodi, a former professor of economics, was frequently satirized in the media as a monotonous bore with a penchant for lulling his audience to sleep. Leaving nothing to chance, the volume offered by Prodi not only outlined cuts in unit labor costs, policies to increase competition and stimulate growth, and measures to reduce the country's debilitating budget deficit, more importantly, it represented an agreement between all members of the center-left Union coalition.

At the beginning of the 2006 campaign, public opinion polls indicated that Prodi and the center-left held a sizeable, though not insurmountable, advantage over Berlusconi and his center-right coalition.[4] Openly suspicious about the pursuit of tax evaders, proposed tax reform and the reintroduction of inheritance taxes, Berlusconi persistently challenged the policy proposals of the center-left. By putting Prodi and the center-left on the defensive with respect to its proposed program, Berlusconi was able to deflect attention away from his rather lackluster performance as prime minister over the last five years. With little to offer the electorate in terms of concrete accomplishments, Berlusconi resorted to insulting the opposition and its supporters, and made more promises of tax cuts and the creation of jobs (Campus 2006b). The most notable promise that he made during the 2006 campaign, and perhaps one of the most memorable campaign promises ever made by any politician in the history of modern democracy, was to abstain from sex in the two-and-a-half months leading up to the election. Unlike his promises of tax cuts and more jobs, this would be one promise that Berlusconi would not have to answer to if it were not kept.

As the election drew near, Berlusconi's comments became more inflammatory and his campaign tactics more desperate. After what was considered a very poor showing in the first of two televised debates, Berlusconi blindsided Prodi in the closing seconds of the second debate with yet another promise: the abolition of the council tax (i.e., local property taxes). Though Prodi was clearly dismayed because the rules and time constraints of the debate did not permit a response, Berlusconi's promise also came as a surprise to some of his own coalition partners.[5] With tensions running high between both sides, Berlusconi would again aggravate Prodi when he backed a warning issued by the U.S. State Department to American tourists in Italy to be prepared for violence in the days and weeks prior to the election. With the warning spurred by an isolated spate of violence that followed a demonstration in Milan by neo-Fascist sympathizers, Berlusconi claimed that the Italian left was once again resorting to political violence and that Italy was facing a "democratic emergency."

In many respects, several of the challenges that Berlusconi faced immediately after he assumed power in 2001 were not of his own making; he was dealt a difficult hand to begin with (i.e., economic recession, constraints imposed by monetary union, and war). Moreover, it is open to debate whether or not the center-left would have fared significantly better if in power during such difficult times. In fact, although Berlusconi's popularity and approval ratings slid precipitously during his premiership, just five years earlier in 2001 it was dissatisfaction with the state of the Italian economy that forced the center-left out and opened the door for the return of *il Cavaliere* (Bellucci 2007). Notwithstanding his control and (ab)use of his media empire to once again create a larger-than-life self-image during the 2006 election campaign, the range of options available to Berlusconi the coalition-builder, the party leader, the billionaire and the patient victim, with which he could respond to and overcome domestic realities and international events were undoubtedly constrained (Pasquino 2007). In this sense, and as we have argued, Berlusconi continues to receive a disproportionate amount of attention with regard to the successes and shortcomings of the center-right. At the same time, Berlusconi's performance and political resilience during the 2006 campaign were quite remarkable. Despite a lackluster record and setbacks in local and European elections, when it mattered most, it is clear that Berlusconi was able to set the agenda during the 2006 election campaign (Campus 2006b). Though he could cite few accomplishments, he remained the undisputed leader of the center-right and of Italy's largest political party, Forza Italia. It was Berlusconi who was able to lead and to put together winning electoral coalitions in 1994 and 2001 and he almost succeeded in doing so again in the 2006 election.

The Electoral Geography of the 2006 Italian National Election

Like the U.S. Presidential election of 2000, the 2006 Italian general election was "too close to call" for some time following the official close of the polls. On April 19, 2006, an Italian court certified Romano Prodi's razor-thin majority in the lower Chamber of Deputies, 49.7 percent for the center-left Union versus 49.4 percent for Berlusconi's center-right coalition, a difference of less than twenty-five

TABLE 5.1   THE 2006 AND 2001 ELECTION
RESULTS FOR THE CHAMBER OF DEPUTIES.

	2006	2001*
House of Freedoms	**49.4**	**49.9**
Forza Italia	23.7	29.4
AN	12.3	12.0
UDC	6.8	3.2
LN	4.6	3.9
Other parties	2.0	1.4
Union	**49.7**	**46.1**
L'Ulivo (DS + Margherita)	31.3	31.1
RC	5.8	5.0
Other parties	12.6	10.0

*Proportional vote. The figures in bold represent the sum/total votes received by each coalition.

thousand votes. Shortly thereafter, another court confirmed Prodi's majority in the Senate, granting the center-left Union 158 seats and Berlusconi's House of Freedoms coalition 156 seats. Refusing to concede defeat, Berlusconi made allegations of electoral fraud and called upon Prodi to form a grand coalition of parties like that of German Chancellor Angela Merkel. Dismissing Berlusconi's demands, Prodi and the center-left Union coalition assumed control of the Italian government in May 2006 at the behest of Italy's new president, Giorgio Napolitano, himself elected by parliament as a whole on largely partisan grounds.

Table 5.1 presents the 2006 election returns from the Chamber of Deputies for the main parties from each coalition. For comparison, the 2001 proportional vote is also included. Recall that between 1993 and 2005 a mixed electoral system was used in Italy in which 75 percent of the seats in the Chamber of Deputies were allocated via plurality in 475 single member districts, and the remaining seats were allocated via proportional representation (PR). Though a new electoral system was recently introduced, the PR component from previous elections permits and facilitates comparisons between 2001 and 2006. One of the most striking features of Table 5.1 is how little the vote share for each coalition changed between 2001 and 2006. Despite evidence that shows a significant increase in swing voting between the two coalitions since 1996 (Bellucci 2007), in 2006, the center-left gained 0.6 percent, and the center-right lost 0.5 percent. However, this apparent stability conceals significant intracoalition shifts—in particular, shifts within the House of Freedoms.

Though Berlusconi's center-right coalition lost only one-half of 1 percent of the vote when compared to its 2001 performance, Berlusconi's party, Forza Italia, suffered a loss of nearly six percentage points. The primary beneficiary of Forza Italia's losses was the Union of Christian Democrats (UDC), now led by Pier Ferdinando Casini. Compared to its 2001 performance in which it received 3.2 percent of the vote, the UDC more than doubled its support in 2006 by obtaining 6.8 percent of the vote. The other key members of the center-right House of Freedoms coalition, the National Alliance and the Northern League, only slightly improved their positions relative to Forza Italia. Just as the coalition vote totals hide intracoalition shifts, national vote totals conceal the geographic distribution of the vote. Table 5.2 breaks down support for the single party that experienced the greatest losses, Berlusconi's Forza Italia, by macroregion. In order to obtain a purchase on the overall electoral-geographic trajectory of Forza Italia, and how it compares to that of the now-disappeared Christian Democrats, returns from the previous four Italian national elections and the 2004 European elections are included. The highest levels of support for Forza Italia are consistently found in the Northwest macroregion, followed by the South, Northeast, and Center, respectively. Shifts in support for Forza Italia between elections are relatively similar for each macroregion,

TABLE 5.2   MACROREGIONAL VOTE SHARE FOR
FORZA ITALIA, 1994–2006.

	Northwest	Northeast	Center	South
DC 1992	25.2	28.8	23.5	39.9
FI 1994	25.2	21.6	17.4	22.3
FI 1996	22.0	16.6	15.8	22.9
FI 2001	29.8	28.3	23.7	30.6
FI (EU elections 2004)	24.3	23.1	18.8	19.1
FI 2006	25.7	22.3	18.6	24.7

with the greatest increases in support occurring between 1996 and 2001 and the greatest decreases occurring between 2001 and 2006. Looking at the latter period in particular, the greatest decreases in Forza Italia support occurred in the South and Northeastern macroregions. Figure 5.1 maps support for Forza Italia in 2006 relative to its performance in 2001 (i.e., FI 2006/FI 2001). Solid black circles represent provinces where support for Forza Italia in 2006 failed to reach 2001 levels, and white circles represent provinces where support for Forza Italia in 2006 exceeded 2001 levels. The size of the circles corresponds to the size of the difference; or in other words, larger circles represent greater differences between 2006 and 2001. Although Forza Italia remained the largest single party in the North and, with the League, provided the foundation upon which national success for the center-right could still be built, two interesting features of a changing electoral geography emerge from this map.[6] First, compared to its 2001 performance, support for Forza Italia in 2006 increased in only five provinces. Moreover, closer investigation reveals that the increases in support in the two southern provinces were less than 1 percent. Second, some of the largest decreases in support occur in Forza Italia's strongholds of Sicily and in the Northeast. In particular, support for Forza Italia decreased by about 10 percent in each of the the three provinces of Agrigento, Ragusa, and Siracusa along the southern coast of Sicily, as well as in the cluster of four provinces west of Venice.

Figure 5.2 complements the previous map by comparing Forza Italia's 2006 intracoalitional vote share to that of 2001 (i.e., [FI 2006/center-right 2006]/[FI 2001/center-right 2001]). This map puts the change in strength of Forza Italia relative to its coalition partners in geographic perspective. Values greater than one denote that Forza Italia's position within the House of Freedoms strengthened since the last election (white circles), values less than one (black circles) indicate that Berlusconi's party has weakened relative to its coalition partners, and the size of the circle denotes the magnitude of the change. Not entirely surprising is the fact that Forza Italia improved its position within the House of Freedoms in only three

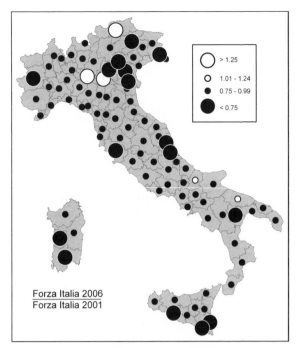

Figure 5.1 Ratio of 2006 Forza Italia support to 2001 Forza Italia support.

Forza Italia 2006
Forza Italia 2001

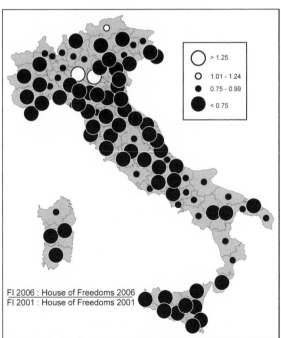

Figure 5.2 Ratio of Forza Italia vote share within the 2006 center-right coalition to Forza Italia vote share within the 2001 center-right coalition.

FI 2006 : House of Freedoms 2006
FI 2001 : House of Freedoms 2001

provinces. However, in all of the remaining provinces, Forza Italia lost ground to its coalition partners, with its greatest setbacks in its stronghold of Sicily.

Figure 5.3 maps the 2006 performance of Gianfranco Fini's National Alliance relative to its performance in 2001. Unlike Forza Italia, the National Alliance gained votes between 2001 and 2006, but not consistently across Italy. The most striking feature was the AN's marked improvement across the North of Italy, in the backyard of both Forza Italia and the Northern League. Fini's party also made headway in Sicily and in Naples as well as in the rural South. However, it is also in the South that the AN lost support in several provinces, and in a few places the post-Fascist party failed to receive more than three-quarters of its 2001 vote share. Fini's attractiveness as a politician—attested to in numerous surveys that gave him higher positive ratings than Berlusconi—and the positioning of AN as a calming and moderate force within the center-right (relative, at least, to the Northern League and Berlusconi) perhaps indicate the final emergence of the party from the political ghetto in which it had been confined hitherto because of its historic attachments to the heritage of Fascism (Fella 2004).

The resurgence of Umberto Bossi's Northern League is also clearly visible in Figure 5.4. Only a handful of provinces register decreases in support between 2001 and 2006. Of course, the League had already suffered a severe erosion of its vote in 2001 relative to 1996. From this viewpoint, 2006 was a maintenance operation more than an expansion. The persisting decline of League support around the city of Milan, however, is particularly notable because this area was once considered a League stronghold and without it any pretense that the League represents an integral "North" is inherently problematic (Agnew et al. 2002). The putative increases of the League elsewhere, are either from very low absolute levels (as in central Italy) or the result of a compact with a local political "boss" (as in the case of the province of Catania in Sicily) (see Chapter 2).

Although Forza Italia remains on the ballot and is in no immediate danger of disappearing from the Italian political landscape, we

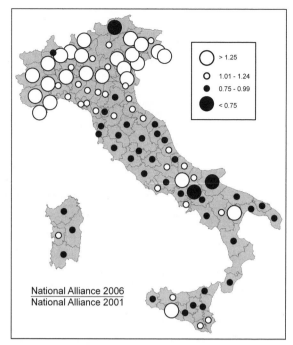

Figure 5.3 Ratio of 2006 National Alliance support to 2001 National Alliance support.

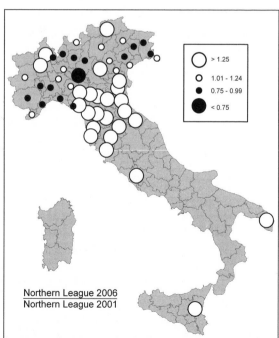

Figure 5.4 Ratio of 2006 Northern League support to 2001 Northern League support.

believe that the party replacement framework used earlier may be useful when examining results for the Union of Christian Democrats (UDC). Like the previous figures, Figure 5.5 compares 2006 UDC electoral performance to that of its predecessors, the former-centrist CCD and CDU. Note that legend values in Figure 5.5 differ from those in previous maps in order to account for the significant increases in support for the UDC. In particular, large white circles denote a minimum twofold increase in electoral support. Furthermore, unlike the previous map of League support, where absolute levels of support in the previous election were very low or did not exist in many places, CCD and CDU support was already relatively modest across Italy in 2001. The UDC made notable gains across the North and Center of Italy, and in several pockets in the South. In fact, only in the hinterland of Milan, in the provinces of Cremona and Mantova, and in a couple of outlying provinces in the South, did support for the centrist-UDC decline.

Although the UDC's gains can be viewed in terms of vote "swings" away from Forza Italia, especially when compared to Figure 5.1, such shifts may also indicate that the UDC is colonizing those areas where Forza Italia once found support. It is clearly premature to conclude definitively that such swings to the UDC are in fact the result of colonization, especially on the basis of just two elections, but it is plausible given the widespread discontent across the center-right with the performance of Berlusconi and his party between the 2001 and 2006 elections. There are surely protest votes involved, but the UDC may be considered by many to be a viable alternative to what has proved to be an ineffective Forza Italia built upon broken promises and vacuous policies. Given Berlusconi's northern bias, the process of colonization may be most apparent across the South where the UDC is recognized as a defender of southern interests. In fact, the greatest percentage increase in UDC support between 2001 and 2006 came from the southern regions of Puglia and Basilicata. Given the withdrawal of Follini and the UDC from Berlusconi's government in 2005, it is clear that some of the former Christian Democrat elements in Italy are trying to distance themselves from Berlusconi and Forza Italia, with the con-

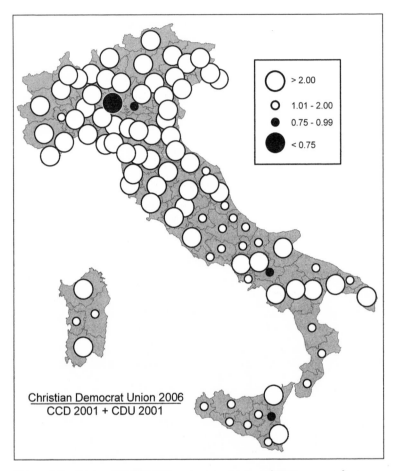

Figure 5.5 Ratio of 2006 UDC support to aggregated 2001 support for former-centrist CCD and CDU.

current objectives of taking votes away from Berlusconi's party (i.e., colonizing) and taking control of the center-right. As Berlusconi and his political promises continue to get old, in both figurative and literal terms, the UDC may be viewed by the Italian electorate as a legitimate political contender, alternative, or even replacement for Forza Italia.

Conclusion

Although the official result from the 2006 Italian general election is recorded as a defeat for the center-right and its leader, the fact that the election was so close, especially after trailing in the polls early on, is a testament to Berlusconi's political acumen and resilience. Spearheading a contentious and at times seemingly desperate campaign that crassly and openly insulted the opposition, offended various segments of the electorate and also alienated himself from his own electoral allies, Berlusconi successfully remained the focal point of the 2006 election. Ultimately refusing to concede defeat in what Prime Minister–elect Romano Prodi called a "strange comedy," Berlusconi's postelection antics in questioning the count and refusing to concede raised just as many questions about his own political future as about Forza Italia and the center-right without *il Cavaliere*. As noted in earlier chapters, explanations of Berlusconi's popularity and success over the last decade frequently emphasize his charisma and the influence of his media empire, which has arguably led to the seemingly inevitable personalization of Italian politics. But as we have shown in this chapter as in previous ones, the machinations of Italian politics continue to rely upon the power plays of political parties with interests that are fundamentally geographic in nature. In other words, the "Berlusconi effect" has been but one component of a political system in which political parties and their respective geographical bases of support continue to shape electoral outcomes.

What is important to understand is that Italian voters experience and interpret their respective social, political, and economic worlds through the geographical lens of living in different places. Moreover, such circumstances as the threat of terrorism, the stagnating economy, and the introduction of the Euro are mediated, experienced, and manifested differently in different places. We believe that the presumed universality of the Berlusconi effect, the personalization of politics, and the role of media and television have been overstated with regard to Italian politics. This is not to say that party organization and politicians are not important—quite the contrary.

But in the end it is the geographical mediation of party activities, political platforms, and voter experiences that matter.

In the five years between the 2001 and 2006 elections, various events and circumstances challenged Berlusconi and the center-right. Although the House of Freedoms is an electoral vehicle par excellence, and few can deny that it has been efficient at collecting votes, we contend that geography played an important role in bringing Berlusconi's House down in 2006. Although united for the election, postvictory issues after 2001 continuously (re)emerged to challenge the efficacy, stability, and image of Berlusconi's leadership, his party, and the center-right coalition at large. Berlusconi was unable to finally mediate or reconcile fundamental differences among his so-called coalition of allies. From the perennial demand for devolution and tax cuts from Bossi's Northern League to the calls for economic stimulus packages for the South made by Fini's National Alliance and Follini's UDC, Berlusconi could do little more than generate publicity—both good and bad—around himself. [7] In light of such divisions within the House of Freedoms, the personalization of Italian politics—in other words, the "Berlusconi effect"—cannot sufficiently explain Italy's most recent electoral outcome. The competing interests of Berlusconi's coalition partners are not only founded upon inherently different views concerning the role of the Italian state but represent fundamentally different, and perhaps incompatible, geographic interests and worldviews. In this regard they reflect real differences between groups of people within the country at large. It remains to be seen whether or not this spells the end, the beginning of the end, or merely an interregnum for Berlusconi's Italy.

6

Conclusion

The closeness of the 2006 election after earlier expectations of an easy center-left victory has reinforced the idea of Berlusconi as Italy's electoral superman. Particularly when seen in the light of the subsequent local elections in May 2006 and the constitutional referendum in June 2006 (when in the absence of much active campaigning by Berlusconi, the center-right appeared unappealing and lost heavily), the role of Berlusconi in turning national elections into referenda about himself seems hard to refute. However, our point is different. Rather than focusing on his leadership as if it entailed an automatic response from an otherwise apathetic electorate, we have emphasized the geographically uneven nature of the "followership" that Berlusconi has stimulated for the center-right. This is the major theme of the book.

Even as Berlusconi has created an electorate for the center-right, it also seems clear that his "toxic" leadership (to borrow a term that has been applied to him by Lipman-Blumen (2006)), while contributing to the polarization of Italian electoral politics into two more-or-less equal bipolar blocs, has also had several other effects. One much noted effect has been to give priority to managing his own legal difficulties over conducting the country's business, particularly its failing economic competitiveness and massive public deficit. During the period from 2001 to 2006, the Berlusconi government did next to nothing to revitalize the Italian economy, leaving the difficult choices to the Prodi government after 2006 (Barber 2006). Without the ability to devalue the currency now that Italy is part of the Eurozone, Italian governments can no longer have recourse to the previously favorite means of reestablishing the competitiveness of the country's exports by lowering prices in foreign currencies. The enormous public debt (107.6 percent of GDP as of 2006) threatens to undermine affiliation with the Euro and disrupt relations with the EU. Doing something serious about it would require no longer pandering to interests, both petty and great, which insist on seeing Italian politics as all about enhancing or protecting their "slice" of the governmental pie (Cartocci 2002; Golden 2003). Another much less noted effect of the toxic leader has been the entrapment of the center-right alliance between the two distinctive geographical coalitions upon which Berlusconi has built his electoral presence since 1994, with the Northern League in the North and with the National Alliance and the UDC (which saw its vote double in 2006 over 2001) everywhere else but particularly in the peninsula South. This is an entrapment because the various elements have persisting policy and personality differences with one another to which Berlusconi has had to devote inordinate attention. If the Northern League and its allies in Forza Italia have had a continuing romance with "devolution" and tax cuts, the other parties in the center-right coalition have wished to either strengthen central government (AN) or while doing this also seek to build once more a "grande spazio al centro" akin to DC (UDC) making them vulnerable to siren songs from their erstwhile colleagues in DC now in the Margherita or elsewhere on the center-left.

Consequently, even with the fragile and unstable center-left government in place as of summer 2007 it is not clear after twelve years as leader of the center-right, with others such as Casini (UDC) and Fini (AN) circling to replace him, that Berlusconi can successfully reinstate his coalition. But absent his particular role, particularly his appeal to those elements in Italian society probably not equally drawn to the leaders of the other center-right parties, it is not clear what would hold the coalition together. As a result, Italy's emerging bipolarity has owed much to Berlusconi, not because of his singularity as a media baron/politician, but because of his ability to put together a geographical "followership" that would otherwise have remained fragmented by party and place.

Place Configurations and Italian Electoral Geography, 1994–2006

Throughout the book we have contrasted two perspectives with our own. If one emphasizes the role of the media (and their Italian maestro, Berlusconi) in creating a single national space for electoral competition, the other focuses on the declining and even residual role of other spatial contexts (regions, in particular) as a variety of social forces (the media, nationwide political preferences, civic traditions, social capital, etc.) help political parties without geographical bases become more or less equally competitive everywhere. The spatial analyses presented in Chapters 3–5 suggest quite strongly that neither of these perspectives readily accounts for what is observed. Rather, what we see are changing or dynamic geographies of electoral turnout and voting for different political parties that can only be explained geographically. We use the term "place configurations" to claim that not only are electoral processes structured geographically but that this happens differentially over time. In other words, the patterns of party expansion and contraction we visually and geostatistically describe cannot be accounted for by fixed national or regional level models of voting. They are best explained by the changing contextual effects of standards of political judgment and affiliation that derive from distinctive identities and interests associated with given places. Sometimes this is very clear. In commenting on how what began as a local dispute over expansion of a U.S. military base erupted into a crisis for the Prodi center-left government in February 2007, Barber (2007) says "Truly, in Italy all politics is local." But sometimes the source is less obviously local or recent. For example, the persisting reluctance to vote for AN in central and northern Italy has much to do with the continuing folk memory of the last days of Fascism between 1943 and 1945 and the disasters it visited on these regions.

As the old party system decayed between the late 1980s and early 1990s, the new parties and the old ones that survived followed different geographical trajectories as they replaced the obsolete ones. If the Northern League colonized old DC strongholds from their margins into the center, the old PCI vote was split between two elements of the old party, the PDS and Refounded Communists, and, most successfully of all, Berlusconi's instant party, Forza Italia, recruited both new voters and a hard-core of old DC voters into its core electorate. The post-Fascist AN and various factions from the DC, such as what later became the UDC and La Margherita, however, took much longer to establish themselves and expand from a relatively low-level presence into a higher profile. We show in considerable detail how the electoral dynamics of the post-1992 Italian Second Republic thus replaced the ancien regime that had been organized for so long between the DC and PCI and a congeries of minor parties in a system incapable of producing governmental bipolarism. The promise of the new arrangements, if not the practice absent a significant majoritarian element in the design of the electoral system, is that a more competitive national politics will also produce more stable national governments and thus better policy commitments and continuity. That electoral bipolarity might consistently produce governmental bipolarism is still more a question of hope than of experience. Putting together coalitions of parties before elections has proven easier than keeping them together afterward.

The Geography of Center-Right "Followership"

The idea of "three Italies" has passed into popular Italian political discourse. The three previous chapters (3–5) have shown in detail how this happened beginning with the Northern League's undermining of established political affiliations before 1992, the subsequent alliances between Forza Italia and the League in the North and Forza Italia and the National Alliance (and a rump of former Christian Democrats) elsewhere, and the emergence of the South as a region of electoral volatility as the Center remained, if weakened, largely a region dominated by the center-left. While having a kernel of truth, we have tried to show how such region-level analysis can be misleading when results are examined more locally. One way of examining how much "the North" has become particularly distinctive in its affiliation with the center-right, beyond the analyses we have already provided, is to look at the results of the constitutional referendum of June 2006. This referendum, resulting from proposals made by the center-right government of 2001–2006, bundled together in one question a number of proposals for changing elements of Part 2 of the Italian Constitution. But this not only provides an interesting opportunity to consider how political attitudes can differ from place to place, it also illustrates how geographical terms, such as "the North" and "the South," "region" and "place," now enter as commonplaces into Italian political discussion. As claimed in Chapter 2 and by example in the other chapters, not only electoral politics but also social and economic differences across the map of Italy can be illustrated by looking closely at the geography of election results, comparing them with the geographical outcomes of previous elections and referenda. Geographical labels, such as "North" and "South," are also inherent in contemporary Italian politics, as they have been in the past with the long-standing focus on the "southern question," which is the economic and political drag exerted on Italy as a whole by an economically underdeveloped South. Today, of course, the question has reversed, with "the North" seemingly calling into question the compact between different regions and the Italian state.

To reiterate one of our most important points, electorates vote according to the opinions they derive from various sources of information as filtered through the basic social and political orientations they acquire during their lifetimes from living and working in different ways in different places (country areas, big cities, small towns, etc.) Obviously, many of the sources of information are no longer primarily local but have become national and global—from newspapers to television. But people are not simply consumers of information whose political behavior is thereafter directed by the media—as much commentary, for example, on Silvio Berlusconi's role in Italian politics claims. People interpret and then disseminate information to others on the basis of political frames of reference picked up and adapted in social interaction with others and also in quiet personal contemplation in the course of everyday life.

The results of the June 2006 referendum illustrate this geographical process of vote determination at work. In the country as a whole the "no" vote prevailed by a large margin (over 60 percent of valid votes). As noted by many commentators, only in northern Italy, and more particularly in Lombardy and the Veneto, did the "yes" vote achieve a majority overall. In the central and southern regions, the "no" vote prevailed almost everywhere by a very large margin, if with much lower turnouts in the South than in the rest of the country, particularly the North. However, left at this, discussion suggests that the geography in question is a simple threefold division of Italy. If the North tended to support the constitutional changes, the Center tended to the "no" side, and the South was vehemently opposed. Certainly, such a geographical simplification into three macroregions has some empirical merit. But it also misses both the fact that the geographical terminology of "North" and "South" is intrinsic to the constitutional changes proposed in the referendum itself (the North stands in for the drive for devolution and the South for continuing centralization) rather than merely a means of collating and comparing results and that there was significant local variation within the three macroregions (particularly noticeable and important politically in the North) suggesting that opinions are not reducible to simple region-wide imperatives.[1]

The proposed constitutional changes, strengthening the office of prime minister at the expense of the president, weakening and federalizing the role of the Senate (currently equal in powers to the Chamber of Deputies), and devolving powers over health, education, and police to the administrative regions, had been pushed through Parliament to please various groups in the center-right government of 2001–2006, above all the Northern League in its demand for weakening the control of Rome over local governments in northern Italy. So, from one perspective, the referendum itself, necessary to achieve public approval of constitutional changes due to slowly go into effect over the next ten years or so, was largely the result of a "northern axis" between Berlusconi's Forza Italia and Umberto Bossi's Northern League. The other two parties in the center-right government, the National Alliance and UDC, electorally anchored in the South, seemed to rouse much less enthusiasm, particularly for devolution, which could be construed as damaging to the South's much greater reliance on central government transfers and lower capacity, because of weaker economic development, to generate revenues to pay for public services locally.

Thus, the referendum itself came about as one way of addressing the now-fabled "northern question" that has become central to Italian politics since the 1980s: the alienation of "the North," more specifically a "profound North" north of the river Po, from Roman government seen as biased in favor of a South ever more dependent on government spending emanating from a productive North ever more lacking in infrastructure and tax incentives to continue its role as the "engine" of Italian economic growth. This theme has been brought forcefully into Italian political discussion primarily by the Northern League but also became an important part of Silvio Berlusconi's political message after 2000. Indeed, the 2006 national election results seemed to indicate considerable public support across northern Italy for this perspective (see Chapters 2 and 5). However, the referendum results suggest that something changed in the northern electorate between April and June 2006. Perhaps moderate voters were offended by Berlusconi's failure to recognize the fact of his electoral defeat and changed sides; or perhaps many of Forza Italia's "nonpolitical" voters (those attracted by the leader rather than by his policies per se) failed to vote in the referendum. From our point of view, it is more likely that only in certain fairly restricted parts of the North is there truly much

strong support for the radical overhaul of the Constitution proposed in the June 2006 referendum.

Let us take, for example, the case of Lombardy. In this region, at
the heart of the North as construed by the Northern League, 54.6
percent of those voting voted "yes" and 45.4 percent voted "no" in
the June 2006 referendum. But these figures mask significant variation within the region (Table 6.1): from 65.4 percent "yes" in the
province of Sondrio to 44.6 percent "yes" in Mantova. Some of this
variation reflects historic attachments (Sondrio lies close to Switzer-
land and inhabitants are well acquainted with localized Swiss approaches to public policy, and Mantova is an area of historic
attachment to the left in an administrative region where this has
been anything but the case in recent years). But even in such well-
established Northern League strongholds as the provinces of Varese
and Lecco, the "yes" vote was under 60 percent. Most significantly,
in the province of Milan, the putative capital of the North as a
whole, the "yes" vote was a scant 50.9 percent. In the capital communes in many provinces the "no" vote prevailed—in eleven out of
nineteen provinces in Lombardy and the Veneto taken together. Indeed, in thirteen out of twenty-three central communes of
provinces in the North where the "yes" vote won (including Milan
and Brescia in Lombardy), the "no" vote was victorious. Thus, the
referendum results sanction the view that rather than indicating a
powerful *regionalism* currently at work in Italian politics, there is an
overwhelming *localism* with different judgments about the so-called
northern question (and what to do about it) in different places
around the North.

When examined geographically, the referendum results bring to
mind various ideas about why some places give rise to patterns of
voting that are distinct from those elsewhere. For example, only in
those largely rural and small-town areas in which the Northern
League has established strong roots did the "yes" vote prevail anywhere in the North. Outside of Lombardy and the Veneto even
these types of places tended to be much more ambivalent about or
antithetical to the proposed constitutional changes. This suggests
some limits to what a politically distinctive "North" actually is and

TABLE 6.1   REFERENDUM OF JUNE 2006. RESULTS IN
THE PROVINCES OF LOMBARDY (% OF VALID VOTES).

	Yes	No
Milan	50.9	49.1
Bergamo	62.7	37.3
Brescia	58.5	41.5
Varese	59.2	40.8
Pavia	52.5	47.5
Como	62.6	37.4
Cremona	53.4	46.6
Mantova	44.6	55.4
Sondrio	65.4	34.6
Lodi	52.6	47.4
Lecco	56.5	43.5

what can be meant by the "northern question." If an imaginative geography is still at the center of Italian politics, then it is increasingly manifested in local rather than regional terms; although processes of social causation are much more multiscalar. As a consequence, there must now be a parting of the ways between the discourse about an expansive "North" that produces economically and desires devolution politically, on the one hand, and a geographical reality across the North in which many parts of it (as Bossi's "Padania" or as something else) can no longer be expected to endorse or support the reduction of Italian politics to a conflict between North and South centered in Rome, on the other. Just as the national election of April 2006 revealed many Souths (with, for example, the center-left becoming dominant electorally in parts of Calabria and Abruzzi), the referendum of June 2006 revealed several Norths, not the least of which is one where the increasingly tattered flag of Padania continues to fly; but now there is scant hope that the Padania in question will ever be anything more than a narrow belt along Italy's northern border. So, even as the referendum results suggest how strongly rooted the Berlusconi/Bossi center-right has become in parts of the North, the North as whole is certainly not without future possibilities for either some other center-right formation or even, in places, for the center-left.

The Geographical Coalitions of the Center-Right

The outcome of the June 2006 referendum also shows the extent to which Berlusconi has had to navigate between the Scylla of the Northern League and the Charybdis of his other partners on the center-right. The 2001–2006 government was widely seen as resting on a Forza Italia–Northern League "axis" which caused considerable irritation with the other coalition partners. On a number of policies there are important differences between the various parties (for example, differences over fiscal policies with varying regional effects, immigration, voting rights for immigrants, and foreign policy). But the FI-League bias seems to have continued beyond the most recent election with Berlusconi seeming to favor his relations with Bossi and the League over his other allies. Cozy dinners with Bossi and other *leghisti* at Arcore, Berlusconi's stately home outside of Milan, seem designed to send a message to the others. This undoubtedly bears some connection to the defection of the League from the first short-lived Berlusconi government and Berlusconi's determination to keep the North (at least the "profound" North) in his column. But it also reflects the fact that Forza Italia and the League are both in origin "northern" movements. Berlusconi's long-term business, sporting, and political ties have always been primarily to Milan. This is the "turf" on which he is most comfortable. At the same time, Bossi and the League have invested heavily in Berlusconi as their partner in their war on Rome. This commitment seems vindicated by the way in which Berlusconi allowed the League to actively participate in government after 2001 but also tolerated the abuse that Bossi (and his minions) directed at his other putative allies in the center-right (Albertazzi and McDonnell 2005).

There is also implicit in Berlusconi's preference for "forzaleghismo" something of a "fear" of the other coalition partners. Today, each is less immediately dependent on Berlusconi than is the League. The UDC could always reach a rapprochement with its former DC colleagues now in the center-left (including Prodi). Indeed, leading exponents of the UDC, such as Marco Follini[2], most vociferously, and Pier Ferdinando Casini, more carefully, have openly called into question Berlusconi's dominance over the center-right. To Follini (2006, 262), Berlusconi represents an Italy:

> that believes little in the virtue of rules and cultivates, if any-thing, a philosophy of success. An Italy that is both localized and Americanized, quick to celebrate the splendors of com-passionate capitalism. An Italy of the belly more than of the head. An Italy, finally, of full-bodied and widespread interests and of habits that are slow to die out and will not be easily erased by the eclipse (sooner or later) of the Cavaliere (Berlusconi).

Casini is typically more circumspect about Berlusconi's toxicity, after all he is the current leader of a party that was, until December of 2006, formally allied with Berlusconi's Forza Italia (and may be again). But he has explicitly questioned the "duality" of Berlus-coni's loyalty, and joked about his political intelligence, by referring to his "two brains" (*Corriere della Sera* 10 May 2006). He also once said that he does "not wish to live and die with Berlusconi," noting that Berlusconi's party performed poorly in 2006, going from 30 to 24 percent of the total vote (relative, for example, to the UDC which went from 3 to 7 percent) and that nowhere in the world is there a democracy in which the same leader in 1994 would still be in place in 2011 (*Corriere della Sera* 6 September 2006).[3] Gianfranco Fini of the AN seems more loyal—at least in public. He does not discourage talk about forming a single party from AN and Forza Italia. But he has a long history of shifting ground on fundamental issues (for example, his view of 1994 that "Mussolini was the great-est statesman of the twentieth century" was later disavowed). Al-though in many opinion surveys he is reported to be the most popular politician in Italy, his telegenic quality and his capacity to take surprising and inconsistent positions serially has led one com-mentator to label him as "the Tony Blair of the right" (the former President, Francesco Cossiga) even as Fini expresses more admira-tion for Jean-Marie Le Pen of the French far-right Front National

(Stella 2005, 109–116). Such political lability and his well-known linguistic opacity might make for a qualified heir to Berlusconi should the latter stumble and fall. Berlusconi has openly endorsed Fini as his successor (*Corriere della Sera* 26 January 2007a) even as he has kept himself constantly in the news by publicly apologizing to his wife for his flirtatious behavior with other women in public (after his wife published a letter in the center-left newspaper *La Repubblica* asking him to do so) and other sorts of theatrical behavior (Romano 2007). Beyond the master himself, the collective memory of Fascism, faded as it may now be, also still provides a problematic legacy for Fini to overcome, particularly in northern and central Italy. AN's improved electoral performance in these regions in 2006 suggests that he may well transcend the specter of Fascism. The Northern League, faded in electoral strength as of 2007, may nevertheless also stand in Fini's way (*Corriere della Sera* 26 January 2007b)

If the center-right as whole suffers from a lack of organizational rootedness in particular places, particularly in Italy's urban areas (Diamanti 2006), it is Forza Italia that still provides what national "glue" there is to keep it together. This is particularly apparent in national elections when the figure of Berlusconi seems especially important in mobilizing voters. The other parties on the center-right have very specific geographical bases. Although Forza Italia also has its very own zone of strength (see Chapters 2, 4, and 5), it is also the only center-right party that stretches across and around the country in its entirety. As in 1994 and in 2006, therefore, absent the linkage provided by Forza Italia, the center-right would likely disintegrate.

Berlusconism After Berlusconi?

Following in the political footsteps of his mentor, Bettino Craxi, Silvio Berlusconi has provided a "middle" party for Italy that has created the possibility of national success for the center-right in Italian national elections by drawing a disparate set of parties together under its rubric. This has moved Italian politics well beyond the Communist-Catholic divide that was the main feature of the party system before 1992 by providing an instrumental or pragmatic party (and politician) that invokes anti-Communism as one of its leitmotifs but offers a very different appeal to the electorate than did the old DC.[4] From this perspective, the center-right does show signs of congealing into something more than just the sum of its parts. This something can be called "Berlusconism."

"Berlusconism" has had as its main components a bluntly instrumental view of electoral politics offered by Forza Italia (a "What can I get out of it?" attitude from both the perspective of the leader and of the voters) and an "entourage" view of the coalition for which Forza Italia has been the glue (Bailey 1988). As Follini suggests, in the quotation given previously, the former element will probably long outlive Berlusconi. His political genius has been to stimulate and tap directly into the instrumentalism of large segments of the Italian electorate. At the same time, Berlusconi has been able to exploit a fundamentally "anti-political" strain in Italian culture to his and his coalition's benefit. The lack of popularity of the 2006 Prodi government only five months after its wafer-thin victory in the April elections was because it had, however inadequately, attempted to wrestle with Italy's serious public-sector deficit and the economy's lack of competitiveness. This example reveals how difficult it will be to wean many Italians away from the expectation of a perpetual "free lunch" that Berlusconi encouraged them to expect as their birthright (on October 2006 poll results, see Mannheimer 2006c). The "entourage" view of the coalition implies that the main allies, while still subordinates, may also have become increasingly interdependent with one another and, in his absence, tempted to slip into the "master's shoes." Some of this acquiescence/challenge is due to Berlusconi's ability to mediate among and persuade his allies to follow his chosen path (Pasquino 2005). But he has also introduced a model of electoral politics to Italy that, in our view, will not be easily excised and that will probably continue even in his absence. One important aspect of this model of electoral politics is captured by the phrase "chequebook democracy" (Hopkin 2005), which implies the development of a candidate-centered politics fueled by funds from businesses, which then demand a quid pro quo in terms of government policies. Although certain aspects of this American approach can be seen as beginning to affect all Italian parties, particularly in the personalized vitriol and negative tactics associated with campaigning, Forza Italia, at least as long as it is dominated by Berlusconi, represents a particularly pathological example of this system. There will always be an inherent conflict of interest involved in protecting Berlusconi's business concerns and patronage, on the one hand, and making national policies, on the other. The other parties on the center-right, particularly AN, would most likely adopt some of the rhetoric and the political logic of Berlusconi of their own accord. Therefore, even as Berlusconi himself may fade from the Italian political scene, his legacy will live on.

Notes

CHAPTER 1   INTRODUCTION: BERLUSCONI'S ITALY

1. Of course, this is to use the standard of the First Republic, at least after 1953, more than such historic precursors as Mussolini, who was famous for his hyperbolic violent language and the allied identification of "enemies within" (Ventrone 2005).

2. Although one important difference is that Republican Party success in the United States until 2006 owed much to the reinvigoration of what is called "retail politics": the use of affiliated organizations, particularly fundamentalist Protestant Churches, whose theology is a peculiar blend of biblical literalism and American nationalism, to enroll new voters to the cause. This harks back to the ways in which the PCI and DC also relied on affiliated organizations to mobilize supporters in the geographical areas in which they were dominant during the heyday of the ancien regime (1950s to 1970s).

3. Sartori (2007) identifies the crux of the issue during the crisis of the Prodi center-left government in February 2007 when he writes: "The Italian problem is not bipolarism at the electoral level (what we call *bipolarity*) but at the level of the government" because of the need to accommodate such a wide ideological range of parties in each coalition. The Berlusconi electoral reform of 2005 with its return to a proportional electoral system exacerbated this problem particularly on the center-left, as it was designed to do. For a detailed examination of how the center-left and center-right differ in their coor-

dination problems, with Berlusconi as the primary mechanism of unity for the latter and the quest for a single party as that of the former, see Diamanti 2007.

4. A more analytic way of putting this would be to say that people must learn different judgment heuristics or yardsticks that they apply to politics as they would in other areas of life. These are socially constructed insofar as they depend on relative exposure to different social contexts and the heuristics they offer (see, e.g., Baldassari 2005). Place-to-place differences in voting behavior are not, therefore, simply reflections of the socioeconomic composition of different places but of the truly contextual differences between places in the political heuristics that prevail.

5. Even if one accepts the overriding power of the media, survey evidence (e.g., ITANES 2001, 116) suggests that it is the Italian center-left rather than Berlusconi and his allies whose electorate is most interested in political messages and thus more open to their content.

6. The massive scale of income-tax evasion in Italy by self-employed businesses and professionals is illustrated by the fact that, according to official figures, dentists in Campania were poorer in 2005 than were policemen and, in Italy as a whole, elementary school teachers were richer than jewelers and owners of cafés (*Corriere della Sera* 13 October 2006). Of course, the policemen and the teachers are taxed as they earn, whereas the others are able to "declare" their incomes on their own behalf. The threat by the center-left government that it intended to investigate tax cheats led many of the beneficiaries of lax enforcement to demonstrate publicly against the government in July and October 2006 (*Corriere della Sera* 13 October 2006).

7. Filippo Sabetti (2000) makes a strong case for the claim that the overly centralized legalism that has characterized modern Italian statehood brings the law into disrepute because there are simply too many unenforceable laws and too little adaptation of those laws to local contexts.

8. Characteristically, when the scandal over fixing games in Italy's Serie A football league broke in the summer of 2006, Berlusconi, as owner of AC Milan, was publicly concerned entirely with how much his club would be punished and not at all with the fact that games had been fixed in the first place (on the scandal, see Turano 2006). When challenged about his monopoly position in commercial television, Berlusconi invariably invokes a marketplace logic to justify it (as if his dominance had been achieved solely by market means!) and accuses his political adversaries of "banditry" when they propose relatively mild measures to encourage diversification of ownership (e.g., *Corriere della Sera* 6 April 2006). Whether to call this "populist" or "patrimonial" (Ginsborg 2007) seems largely beside the point; it is an instrumental conception of the purpose of national politics that has long had a wide if geographically differential appeal across Italy (and indeed elsewhere) (Sapelli 1994, 1997).

CHAPTER 2   THE GEOGRAPHY OF
THE NEW BIPOLARITY, 1994–2006

1. By way of a recent example of research taking the instrumental character of Italian electoral politics seriously, Miriam Golden (2003) persuasively argues that historically in postwar Italy (1948–1994) many people looked to elections as a potential counterweight to the failings of government bureaucratic transparency or rule-based delivery of public services and thus expected something of a material reward from their political representatives in return for their votes. This strongly supports the logic of political instrumentalism introduced in Chapter 1. Not only did this type of electoral process encourage voters to look locally for their rewards but also led to geographical variation in patterns of delivery of patronage depending upon which parties, factions within parties, and individual politicians within a given government controlled a specific department or ministry.

2. Some reviews of Agnew (2002), for example, insist on keeping "place" at a single, fixed scale, as equivalent to the locality (e.g., Petrusewicz 2004; Dainotto 2005). In this usage, if Putnam (1993) prefers regions, then Agnew prefers localities. Of course, this means missing the entire point about the geographical dynamics that not only separate places but also necessarily tie them together as well.

3. However, we should make clear that Diamanti's overall body of work is a good example of the focus on geographical variation that we are advocating in this book. Our differences with some of his more recent analysis of the historical-geographical course of that variation should not be understood as criticism of his work tout court. We admire his research record greatly and would not wish to give any other impression. This is a disagreement among close intellectual allies, not a conflict of adversaries à la Berlusconi!

4. Even when there is evidence of the impact of media bias on voting (e.g., Della Vigna and Kaplan 2006 on the impact of the extreme right-wing Fox News in the United States on the 2000 and 2004 presidential and Senate elections) the impact varies significantly depending on place characteristics (urban/rural, north/south, ethnic composition, etc.) suggesting that a range of nonmedia mediating factors are at work in translating media messages into electoral outcomes.

5. From this viewpoint, the center-left DS-Margherita grouping is as "ungrounded" as Forza Italia in contemporary Italian politics. Indeed, its leader, Romano Prodi, was not in 2006 a member of any of the constituent parties! But given the ideologically "maximalist" character of the Italian far left, coalition building on the center-left is harder than it is on the center-right (Sartori 2006b).

6. Berlusconi's ability to mobilize many so-called apolitical voters in national elections does contrast with Forza Italia's often lackluster performance in local elections (as in May 2006, Diamanti 2006c) and when Berlusconi is less visible politically (as during the campaign for the constitutional referendum in June 2006). One of his political allies of the centrist UDC, Rocco Buttiglione, put down the failure of the "yes" vote after the referendum to the increasingly "ephemeral" territorial nature of the center-right's relationship to its electorate (Buttiglione TG1 26 June 2006). But outside some of the center-left's strongholds in central Italy it is not clear that it is any better grounded locally. Even there, the "golden age" seems to have passed (Ramella 2005). In 2001, for example, the center-right did better among housewives in traditionally "red" central Italy than in Italy as a whole in the majoritarian part of the election: 64.2 to 60.0 percent (Ramella 2005, 200). Housewives are often seen as a quintessential Berlusconi constituency because they watch relatively more television than other social groups. More likely, the medium is not the message. Rather, it is because Berlusconi appeals to the importance of their social role and to their fantasies of the "good life" and to those of others of the very large number of Italians not in full-time formal or tax-paying employment (pensioners, part-time employees, self-employed) whereas the center-left has a language and appeal directed almost entirely to those in salaried employment. The conversations and other social interactions of everyday life ignite and reinforce such differential affiliations. The old party system never offered much to this type of voter, so Berlusconi acquired something of a "base" among them and those who benefit from lax enforcement of laws on land use and tax evasion (e.g., Salvati 2003, 574).

7. Berlusconi's accusation after the narrow defeat of his coalition in 2006 that "irregularities" in the voting had deprived him of victory and thus delegitimize his opponents suggests not only a paranoid cast of mind (after all, the election was organized by his Minister of the Interior) but that *his* persecution complex is not simply strategic. His frequent recourse to violent and vulgar language, particularly characteristic of his 2006 election campaign, if sometimes disavowed immediately after delivery, reflects perhaps both the long-term success of the language of "enemies" in Italian political discourse (Ventrone 2005) and the more recent turn to vulgarity associated above all with the Northern League and its leader, Umberto Bossi, as indicating the honesty of an "everyman" and as an alternative to the duplicity of "typical" politicians.

8. In his classic work, *Political Parties*, Maurice Duverger (1964, 179) noted the importance of "personal leadership" for those parts of the population incapable of framing politics in terms of institutions and ideologies. Survey research in Italy in 2005 shows that close to half of those interviewed had a worse impression of Italian politicians than of Italians in general (Vignati

2006, 147). This makes them very open to populist appeals from "anti-politician" politicians (see Mastropaolo 2000 and Tarchi 2003). Berlusconi was successful in 2006 in appealing to "his" Italy by demonizing another alien and, among other things, "communist" one. This strategy of designating "two Italies" has been vital in both creating bipolarity and making it a war between social enemies rather than conflict between respectful political adversaries (Berselli and Cartocci 2006).

9. This "civil society" is not always as civil or as progressive as sometimes made to seem. Chambers and Kopstein (2001), for example, provide a useful general corrective in this regard to those who selectively focus on various charitable and progressive groups as invariably positive in challenging or replacing the dead hand of party politics in Italy (e.g., Putnam 1993; Ginsborg 2004b; Andrews 2005).

10. For a thorough examination of the idea of "nationalization" of electorates and what it does or does not signify about the voting process, see Caramani (1994). In his recent book (Caramani 2004), he seems to have forgotten much of this, perhaps because of his reorientation to an Anglo-Saxon political-science readership.

11. Opinion polls before the 2006 election and exit polls during the election proved relatively inaccurate in forecasting the close outcome of the election. This probably had something to do with the number of undecideds and "reticents" but also seems to have reflected respondents often saying that they intended to vote for or did vote for DS and then voted for one of the parties in the center-right coalition (Jampaglia 2006; Sottocornola 2006). The increase in the number of last-minute undecided voters, however, probably helped Berlusconi more than the center-left, if only because he had "clearer" signals directed at the material interests of many of them. According to the political logic identified by Feddersen and Pesendorfer (1999), the "noisy signal" from the center-left (given the diverse array of parties) would drive down turnout among their (weak) sympathizers.

12. Although, as Fabbrini (2005, 67) suggests, if the "consensual democracy" of the First Republic is well in the past, "that of competition still isn't close. And the stability of the government is something other than guaranteed, notwithstanding the strengthening of institutions and the growing leadership of the prime minister."

13. Whether this electoral system will remain in place is moot as of August 2007. It was designed specifically to enhance the prospects of the center-right government winning the April election of 2006. It is unlike any electoral system anywhere else in the world in combining elements (Senate seats allocated at a regional level, Chamber seats at the national level; "topping up" of seats for winning coalitions; and seats reserved for voters outside the country) that seem to offer no pretense at fairness and, as a result, were imposed by the

center-right majority even though the existing system had been endorsed by popular referendum in 1993 in preference to a PR system. After his victory in 1994, Berlusconi had declared that the majoritarian system was his "religion." To reduce the prospects for governability by others in his absence from power, Berlusconi was willing to sacrifice the very system that had helped bring bipolarity to Italian politics (Stille 2006). On the new electoral system's specific characteristics and for a brilliant simulation of how the differential organization of the Chamber and Senate elections was likely to produce the impasse in 2006 that it did, see D'Alimonte and Chiaramonte (2006).

14. The Refounded Communists registered a net national increase of 0.7 percent in 2006 over 2001 in its vote for the Chamber of Deputies to become the sixth largest party overall and the third on the center-left (5.7 percent and 41 seats).

15. Notwithstanding much talk about mergers between DS and Margherita on the center-left and Forza Italia and the National Alliance on the center-right, not much actually came of this except the decision to run candidates of the aforementioned two parties in Chamber contests in 2006 under the sign of L'Ulivo, formerly the name of the center-left coalition as a whole. As of summer 2007, however, a new Democratic party for the center-left is actively under construction.

16. Although there was a strong positive correlation between votes in the SMDs and the PR contests—in that there was not a large "leakage" of votes between one coalition in the former and affiliated parties of the other in the latter—the center-left tended to perform better than its constituent parties and vice versa for the center-right. In 2001 only four hundred thousand votes separated the coalitions nationally in the SMDs, while 3.3 million more voters preferred the House of Freedoms parties in the PR ballot (Parker and Natale, 2002: 669). Much of this "gap" was either due to more center-leftists voting for noncoalition parties in the PR part, or to higher rates of abstention on their part in PR contests, rather than a shift across coalitions between the two parts of the election.

17. In his careful empirical analysis of the outcomes of Berlusconi's 2001 "Contract with Italians," Ricolfi (2006) shows that the center-right did not have much justification in campaigning in 2006 as if it had achieved much success in the areas of tax reform and public works during its five years of government. Indeed, it could be said that the contract itself was more leftwing, in its emphasis on pensions and job growth, than it was rightwing (in a neoliberal sense), ignoring completely such matters as privatization of state assets, liberalization of labor markets, and reducing the government deficit (see, e.g., Cazzola 2005). From this viewpoint, voting for the center-right in 2006 can hardly be construed as validating retrospective voting along economic lines!

18. Indeed, it is reasonable to refer to a "forzaleghista" ideology and rhetoric as the main feature of Berlusconi's electoral campaign in 2006, reflecting the dominance of this northern axis over the other elements in the center-right coalition (Berselli and Cartocci 2006; Follini 2006).

19. This need to please different clienteles within the coalition is also apparent in the concurrent attempt to both strengthen the role of the prime minister and devolve some governmental powers to the administrative regions in the legislation passed by the center-right government in November 2005 and subject to a single referendum vote in June 2006. This packaging together of diverse constitutional changes and the changes themselves have been subject to devastating critique by many legal scholars and political scientists (Elia 2006). Much of the nationwide electorate, save for significant numbers in Lombardy and the Veneto attracted most by the prospect of devolution, seemed to agree that the proposals were something of a mess and voted "no" in an overwhelming proportion that increased (if with lower turnouts) from north to south (see Chapter 6).

CHAPTER 3   PARTY REPLACEMENT, ITALIAN STYLE

1. This collapse of the "first" and the subsequent emergence of the so-called "second" Italian republic is well documented (e.g., Bartolini and D'Alimonte, 1995; D'Alimonte and Bartolini, 2002; Diamanti and Mannheimer, 1994; Gangemi and Riccamboni, 1997; Gundle and Parker, 1996). Most attention, however, has been given to either why the old system collapsed (the end of the cold war, the activism of the judiciary in Milan in prosecuting corruption by the old parties, the breakdown of the system of sharing the spoils of government, etc.) or to specific features of what followed: the new electoral system of 1993 (e.g., D'Alimonte and Chiaramonte 1995; Pappalardo 1995); the role of Italy's wealthiest businessman, Silvio Berlusconi, in the new party system (e.g., McCarthy 1996); the difficulty of creating a united left from left-Catholic and Communist fragments (e.g., Cartocci 1994; Ignazi 1992); the disruptive character of Umberto Bossi's Northern League (e.g., Diamanti 1993, 1996); and the rehabilitation of the far right in Italian politics (e.g., Tarchi 1997).

2. Note that results from spatial analyses use election returns from the proportional representation (PR) component of the 1994, 1996 and 2001 Italian national elections. Recall that a mixed PR/majoritarian electoral system was introduced in 1993, and was subsequently abolished in October 2005 in favor of a return to a PR. Since our particular interest is in how old parties were replaced, and not necessarily voter transitions between concurrent elections (e.g., see Wellhofer (2001)), we are restricted to using the PR element because it permits comparability between the old (pre-1993) and new (post-1993) party

systems. The data, provided by the Cattaneo Institute in Bologna and reported at the level of the Italian municipality (N > 8,000), were aggregated up to the level of Italian provinces. Eight new provinces have been introduced over the course of the study period, but to facilitate consistent spatial and temporal comparisons, the 1987 Italian provincial configuration is maintained for the entire analysis. Note also that the region of Val d'Aosta is excluded from the analysis because it is a single member constituency and does not elect a deputy using PR.

3. The classic indicator used to identify the presence of spatial autocorrelation is Moran's I (e.g., see Cliff and Ord 1981; Griffith 1987). Moran's I can be expressed as: $\Sigma_i\Sigma_j w_{ij}(x_i - \mu)(x_j - \mu) / \Sigma_i(x_i - \mu)^2$, where w is an element in a row-standardized spatial weights matrix, W, that summarizes the geographic linkages between observations (i.e., 1 = adjacency; 0 = separation), x is the vote share for the party of interest, and μ is the average vote share for the party of interest. Contiguity or adjacency is used to capture the geographic relations between provinces in the spatial weights matrix W. Other methods exist to fill such weights matrixes (e.g., selection of a cut-off distance), but contiguity is useful here because it corresponds to the minimum distance between provinces, and serves as a good surrogate for local-level interdependencies.

4. The equation for the local Moran's I index is: $z_i / \Sigma z_i^2 \Sigma w_{ij}z_j$, where z is measured in deviations from the mean and inference is based upon a conditional randomization method (see Anselin 1995a, b).

CHAPTER 4   THE GEOGRAPHICAL SECRET
TO BERLUSCONI'S SUCCESS

1. In terms of his logic of "strategems and spoils" Bailey (2001) would see these people as those who benefit most from a pragmatic application of rules rather than those who appreciate more transparent application of rules on the basis of, say, merit, justice, equality, etc. (see Berselli and Cartocci 2006) for the distinction between a "real" Italy devoted to such pragmatism and an "imagined" Italy of transparent rule application). One of Bailey's main points would be that Italy is hardly singular in this regard.

2. Whether this is that recent, however, seems very doubtful both with respect to the historic importance of *trasformismo* (or vote trading between representatives) and long-standing low levels of "public trust" and high levels of tolerance of corruption (petty and otherwise) reported in many opinion surveys (see, e.g., Cartocci 1994; 2002).

3. Much popular commentary on the politics of the center-right coalition (e.g., Andrews 2005; Diamanti and Lello 2005; Stille 2006) overstates the distinctions between the various parts of the coalition without identifying

what brings them together other than the force of Berlusconi's personality, his media control, or their desire to avoid the political "wilderness." If Stille (2006) does show the importance of Craxi as the "godfather" of the new center-right it is more in terms of Berlusconi's initial recruitment into national politics rather than with respect to the continuation of the PSI strategy under new auspices. The tortuous attempts of Berlusconi to both escape from yet acknowledge the crucial role of Craxi in his rise to power is illustrated in the quotations from "Il Cavaliere" in the first few pages of the hilarious book by Marco Travaglio (1995, 2–4).

4. Stille (2006, 266) quotes the Milan chief prosecutor of corruption crimes, Francesco Saverio Borelli, to the effect that, beginning in 1993, it was the crackdown on tax evasion among the general public that led to declining support for prosecuting more high-profile perpetrators. Berlusconi's troubles with the judiciary thus struck a sympathetic chord with many people afraid that they might be investigated (and possibly found guilty) rather than simply outraging them.

5. The center-left, however, has also retained an "old left" emphasis on paid employees as its primary constituency, potentially alienating those, such as housewives and artisans, whose dreams and interests have been more readily exploited by Berlusconi (see Chapter 2).

6. The leaders of the parties continued to rail against one another up until the last moment before declaring their alliances, suggesting how instrumental they were in "burying the hatchet." For example, as late as February 1, 1994, Umberto Bossi of the League had said "Never in government with the Fascist pigsty [AN]," and Gianfranco Fini of AN said the next day: "Occhetto [of PDS] is the adversary, Bossi [of the League] is the enemy. We will never accept any technical agreement with the League" (see, for more of these and other contradictory sayings of the leaders of the center-right at the time, Travaglio 1995).

7. Plausibly, on the basis of surveys of how political preferences are established, southern voters have been characterized more than voters elsewhere in Italy as perceiving their votes instrumentally relative to the redistributive potential and likelihood of achieving office of specific parties. Consequently, as judgments can be made only on the basis of previous experience, it is only once parties have acquired office and provided evidence of redistributive intentions that votes will drift in their direction (Ricolfi 1994, 588). Interestingly, and supportive of the "Craxi-Berlusconi thesis," many PSI voters in 1992 became FI voters right off the bat in 1994 (Mannheimer 1994, 32; Biorcio 1994, 162).

8. Beyond the question of the distinctive basis to the "followership" of Forza Italia relative to DC, Hopkin (2005) suggests that the new party represented the birth of a "chequebook democracy" in Italy with some

analogy to the candidate, fund-raising, and lobbying nexus of U.S. electoral politics.

9. Bossi showed his gratitude by spending much of the campaign attacking his ally Berlusconi by associating him with the old regime (Diamanti 1994, 56). The hostility was only to intensify after the 1994 election until a sudden rapprochement in 2000, reversed the major switch of the League's program to secessionism and opposition to "Roman politics" of the intervening years.

10. Ever since, D'Alema has been Berlusconi's "favorite" politician on the center-left!

11. Appearing on the RAI 1 program *Porta a Porta* one week before the 2001 election, showing a single page that looked exactly like a legal contract, Berlusconi laid out the following "promises" for his future term in office, if elected: 1) reducing all taxes to a maximum of 33 percent of income, 2) a major reduction in crime, 3) raising minimum pensions to a million lire per month, 4) cutting the unemployment rate in half and adding a million new jobs, 5) starting 40 percent of a ten-year plan of major public works. The failure to come anywhere close on most of these did not discourage Berlusconi from running for office again in 2006 (see Ricolfi 2006).

12. By this date, various political forces, not the least of which were the center-left governments of the 1990s, had already initiated considerable "devolution" of power, chiefly to the regional level, particularly in relation to health services (see Parker 2006). Bossi was looking for something "symbolic" to associate the League with after the failure of Padania to attract positive attention in most of the North, particularly in the main metropolitan areas. Others had already stolen his political clothes, so to speak.

CHAPTER 5   WHAT WENT UP LATER CAME DOWN

1. One of the key themes of recent revisionist thinking about the Italian South is that the "region" has always been much more internally diverse economically and politically than the conventional discourse of *meridionalismo* (the study of the South predominantly by Northerners) has made it seem (see, e.g., Lumley and Morris 1997).

2. The architect of the electoral change, the Northern League's Roberto Calderoli, later famously described his proposal as a *porcata* (meaning "a piece of crap," or "dirty trick"). Ironically, the House of Freedoms was hoist on its own petard when the center-left turned out to be the beneficiary of the two most important "reforms": the topping-up of seats in the Chamber for even a small majority of total votes and the extension of the franchise to Italians resident abroad (Messina 2006). Notwithstanding the outcome, however, the new electoral system undoubtedly represents a backward step in the process of stabilizing bipolarism within the Italian political system (Berselli 2006).

3. Even more than in previous national elections, Berlusconi relied on emotional appeals to voters to reduce dissonance relating to his failure to deliver on the "Contract with Italians." Nothing was said about that. Instead, he inflated promises almost to the level of fantasy and focused on the presumed negatives of his opponents using the language of political friends and enemies rather than allies and adversaries (see, e.g., Ostellino 2006; *Corriere della Sera* 6 April 2006). On the uses of emotional appeals in politics to reduce cognitive dissonance when interests have been questionably served (see Brader 2006).

4. Throughout January and February 2006, however, polls showed a slow erosion of the center-left vote (see, e.g., Mannheimer 19 January 2006; Mannheimer 21 February 2006).

5. There is survey evidence which suggests that this promise was important in mobilizing a portion of the electorate generally ill-disposed toward parties and politicians but eager for some reward for their votes (see Riotta 2006; ISPO 2006). Milan may be the capital of such sentiments (Galli della Loggia 2006).

6. It is important to reemphasize that the North remains the region in which the center-right's national success remains anchored as does central Italy for the center-left. Panebianco (2006) claims that the center-left remains largely unable to understand the popular antistatism upon which both the League's and Forza Italia's popular appeal largely rests. It thus remains estranged from much of the largest "reservoir" of voters in the country. But this undoubtedly understates the degree to which salaried workers and those committed to more transparent government (wherever they are) find themselves outvoted by those for whom government is both a shield and an enemy. Italy's peculiar tragedy is in having so many of the latter (see Chapters 1, 2, and 4).

7. This has continued after the 2006 election irrespective of the difficulties into which the Prodi government has run (Diamanti 28 June 2006). However, Berlusconi's penchant for political theater and his capacity to draw attention to himself by outrageous behavior or tasteless expression remain a resource for his allies; and, ironically, because it seems unserious, this behavior narrows the political divide that would otherwise be much wider throughout the country (Berselli and Cartocci 2006).

CHAPTER 6   CONCLUSION

1. The use of the macroregional labels also lends itself to a reproduction of long established political stereotypes such as those about a "parasitic" and "patronage ridden" South versus a politically virtuous North around which much ot the Northern League's discourse has tended to circulate. Yet, as we have argued throughout this book, there is much evidence that political

instrumentalism is not so easily regionalized. Indeed, in recent years new political movements oriented to local disputes are as evident in southern places as they are elsewhere (e.g. Zinn 2007).

2. In October 2006 Follini announced that he was leaving the UDC because it had not abandoned the center-right coalition led by Berlusconi (La Repubblica 10 October 2006; *Corriere della Sera* 18 October 2006). Later in the year the UDC did just that (*Corriere della Sera* 4 December 2006).

3. Rocco Buttiglione, chairman of the UDC (*La Repubblica*, 14 September 2006) has compared Berlusconi to Carl Schmitt (the Nazi philosopher) because of his tendency to see politics in terms of a struggle to the death between friends and enemies; whereas Buttiglione and the UDC saw politics, following the view of Pope John Paul II, as defining a "common good." The desire for reestablishing a "big center" for Italian politics still inspires many former Christian Democrats such as Buttiglione. Roberto Maroni, number two in the Northern League, openly worried in late October 2006 that the center-right coalition faced disintegration and that the League might do better alone (*La Repubblica* 23 October 2006). The League itself faces the prospect of major scission because, in the words of one critic in a League stronghold (Varese), it has become a "prosthesis" of Forza Italia (Varese Laghi, 5 November 2006).

4. Although the center-right has certainly not been averse to using issues important to the Vatican and the Catholic Church (such as fertility treatments, end-of-life controversies, abortion, and civil rights for homosexuals) as tools for mobilizing public opinion on its behalf (Diamanti and Ceccarini 2007).

References

Agnew, J. 1987a. *Place and politics: The geographical mediation of state and society.* London: Allen & Unwin.

————. 1987b. Place anyone? A comment on the McAllister and Johnston papers. *Political Geography Quarterly* 6: 39–40.

————. 1988. Better thieves than Reds? The nationalization thesis and the possibility of a geography of Italian politics. *Political Geography Quarterly* 7: 307–321.

————. 1992. Place and politics in post-war Italy: A cultural geography of local identity in the provinces of Lucca and Pistoia. In Anderson, K., and F. Gale, eds., *Inventing places: Studies in cultural geography.* Melbourne: Longman Cheshire.

————. 1995. The rhetoric of regionalism: The Northern League in Italian politics, 1983–1994. *Transactions of the Institute of British Geographers* 20: 156–172.

————. 1996. Mapping politics: How context counts in electoral geography. *Political Geography* 15: 129–146.

————. 1997. The dramaturgy of horizons: geographical scale and the reconstruction of Italy by the new Italian political parties, 1992–1995. *Political Geography* 16: 99–121.

————. 2002. *Place and politics in modern Italy.* Chicago: University of Chicago Press.

Agnew, J., M.E. Shin, and G. Bettoni. 2002. City versus metropolis: The Northern League in the Milan metropolitan area. *International Journal of Urban and Regional Research* 26: 266–283.

Agnew, J., M. Shin, and P. Richardson. 2005. The saga of the second industrial divide and the history of the third Italy: Evidence from export data. *Scottish Geographical Journal* 121: 83–101.

Albertazzi, D., and D. McDonnell. 2005. The Lega Nord in the second Berlusconi government: in a league of its own. *West European Politics* 28: 952–972.

Alesina, A. and F. Criavazzi. 2007. *Il Liberaslimo è di sinistra.* Milan: Il Saggiatore.

Anderson, P. 2002. Land without prejudice. *London Review of Books*, 21 March.

Andreucci, F., and Pescarolo, A. 1989. La formazione delle regioni rossi in Italia: il caso di Toscana. In F. Andreucci, and A. Pescarolo, eds. *Gli spazi di potere. Aree, regioni, Stati: le coordinate territoriali della storia contemporanea.* Florence: Usher.

Andrews, G. 2005. *Not a normal country: Italy after Berlusconi.* London: Pluto Press

Anselin, L. 1988. *Spatial econometrics: methods and models.* Dordrecht: Kluwer Academic.

———. 1989. What is special about spatial data? Alternative perspectives on spatial data analysis. In *Symposium on spatial statistics, past, present and future.* Syracuse, NY.: Department of Geography.

———. 1992. *Spatial data analysis with GIS: An introduction to application in the social sciences.* Santa Barbara CA: National Center for Geographic Information Analysis (NCGIA).

———. 1995a. Local indicators of spatial association—LISA. *Geographical Analysis* 27: 93–115.

———. 1995b. *SpaceStat, version 1.80 user's guide.* Morgantown, WV: Regional Research Institute.

Augias, N., and A. Covotta. 2005. *I cattolici e l'Ulivo. Sfogliando la Margherita.* Rome: Donzelli.

Baccetti, C. 1997. *Il Pds.* Bologna: Il Mulino.

Bailey, F.G. 1988. *Humbuggery and manipulation: The art of leadership.* Ithaca: Cornell University Press.

———. 2001. *Stratagems and spoils: A social anthropology of politics* (revised edition). Boulder: Westview.

Baldassari, D. 2005. *La semplice arte di votare. Le scorciatoie cognitive degli elettori italiani.* Bologna: Il Mulino

Barbagallo, F. 1994. *La modernità squilibrata del Mezzogiorno d'Italia.* Turin: Einaudi.

Barber, T. 2006. System failure: a coalition creaks as Prodi's chance to reform slips away. *Financial Times*, 30 October: 1.

Barber, T. 2007. Reform hopes recede as intrigue grips the Italian patient. *Financial Times*, 23 February: 11.

Bartolini, S., A. Chiaramonte, and R. D'Alimonte. 2004. The Italian party system between parties and coalitions. *West European Politics* 27: 1–19.

Bartolini, S., and R. D'Alimonte. 1994. La competizione maggioritario: Le origini elettorali del Parlamento diviso. *Rivista Italiano di Scienza Politica*, 24: 631–686.

———. eds. 1995. *Maggioritario ma non troppo*. Bologna: Il Mulino.

Bellucci, P. 2007. Changing models of electoral choice in Italy. *Modern Italy* 12: 55–72.

Bendicenti, D. 2006. La televisione e la campagna elettorale permanente. *Il Mulino* 423: 56–63.

Benoit, K., M. Laver, D. Giannetti. 2004. Multiparty split-ticket voting estimation as an ecological inference problem. In G. King et al. eds. *Ecological inference: New methodological strategies*. Cambridge: Cambridge University Press.

Berselli, E. 2006. Che cosa è in gioco il 9 aprile. *Il Mulino* 423: 27–33.

Berselli, E. and R. Cartocci, 2001. Il bipolarismo realizzato. *Il Mulino* 395: 449–460.

———. 2006. Due Italie, forse. A proposito delle elezioni del 9–10 aprile. *Il Mulino* 424: 243–52.

Biorcio, R. 1994. Le ragioni della sinistra. Le risorse della destra. In I. Diamanti and R. Mannheimer, eds. *Milano a Roma: Guida all'Italia elettorale del 1994*. Rome: Donzelli.

Bobbio, N. 1996. *Left & right: The significance of a political distinction*. Cambridge: Polity.

Bodei, R. 2006. *We, the divided: Ethos, politics and culture in post-war Italy, 1943–2006*. New York: Agincourt.

Bogaards, M. 2005. The Italian First Republic: degenerated consociationalism in a polarized party system. *West European Politics* 28: 503–20.

Books, J., and C. Prysby. 1991. *Political behavior and the local context*. New York: Praeger.

Brader, T. 2006. *Campaigning for hearts and minds: How emotional appeals in political ads work*. Chicago: University of Chicago Press.

Brusa, C. 1984. *Geografia elettorale nell'Italia del dopoguerra. Edizione aggiornata ai risultati delle elezione politiche 1983*. Milan: Unicopli.

Bull, M.J., and J.L. Newell. 2006. *Italian politics: Adjustment under duress*. Cambridge: Polity.

Bull, M. and G. Pasquino. 2007. A long quest in vain: Instiutional reforms in Italy, *West European Politics*, 30: 670–91.

Burnham, W.D. 1970. *Critical elections and the mainsprings of American politics.* New York: Norton.

Butler, D., and D. Stokes. 1969. *Political change in Britain.* New York: St. Martin's.

Buttiglione, R. 2006. Comments on TG1 in aftermath of referendum of 25–26 June 2006.

Butz, W. P., and B. B. Torrey. 2006. Some frontiers in social science. *Science* 312 (30 June): 1898–1900.

Caciagli, M., and A. Spreafico. 1990. *Vent'anni di elezioni in Italia. 1968–1987.* Padova: Liviana.

Calvo, E., M. Escolar. 2003. The local voter: A geographically weighted approach to ecological inference. *American Journal of Political Science* 47: 189–204.

Campus, D. 2006a. *L'antipolitica al governo. De Gaulle, Reagan, Berlusconi.* Bologna: Il Mulino.

————. 2006b. The 2006 election: more than ever, a Berlusconi-centred campaign. *Journal of Modern Italian Studies* 11: 516–531.

Cannari, L., and G. D'Alessio. 2003. La distribuzione del reddito e della richezza nelle regioni italiane. *Temi di discussione.* Rome: Banca D'Italia.

Cannari, L. and S. Chiri. 2004. La bilancia dei pagamenti di parte corrente Nord-Sud 1998–2000. *Temi di discussione.* Rome: Banca D'Italia.

Caramani, D. 1994. La nazionalizzazione del voto. *Rivista Italiana di Scienza Politica* 24: 237–85.

————. 2004. *The nationalization of politics: The formation of national electorates and party systems in Western Europe.* Cambridge: Cambridge University Press.

Cartocci, R. 1990. *Elettori in Italia.* Bologna: Il Mulino.

————. 1994. *Fra Lega e Chiesa.* Bologna: Il Mulino.

————. 2002. *Diventare grandi in tempi di cinismo. Identità nazionale, memoria collettiva, e fiducia nelle istituzioni tra I giovani italiani.* Bologna: Il Mulino.

————. 2004. Il bipolarismo reale. *Il Mulino* 411: 57–66.

————. 2007. *Mappe del tesoro. Atlante del capitale sociale in Italia.* Bologna: Il Mulino.

Castagnoli, A., ed. 2004. *Culture politiche e territorio in Italia, 1945–2000.* Milan: Franco Angeli.

Cazzola, F. 1992. *L'italia del pizzo. Fenomenologia della tangente quotidiana.* Turin: Einandi.

Cazzola, G. 2005. Governo di destra, politiche di sinistra. *Il Riformista.*

Chambers, S. and J. Kopstein. 2001. Bad civil society. *Political Theory* 29: 837–865.

Chiaramonte, A. 2002. Il voto proporzionale: verso la nazionalizzazione della competizione? In R. D'Alimonte and S. Bartolini. eds. *Maggioritario finalmente? La transizione 1994–2001.* Bologna: Il Mulino.

Cho, W.T. 2003. Contagion effects and ethnic contribution networks. *American Journal of Political Science* 47: 368–387.

Cliff, A., and J. Ord. 1981. *Spatial processes: models and applications.* London: Pion Limited.

Corriere della Sera. 6 April 2006. Berlusconi: Non credo tanti coglioni.

———. 10 May 2006. Casini e la teoria dei due cervelli di Silvio.

———. 6 September 2006. Non voglio vivere e morire con Berlusconi.

———. 13 October 2006a. Professionisti in piazza contro il governo.

———. 13 October 2006b. I gioiellieri guadagnano meno dei maestri.

———. 4 December 2006. Casini: La casa delle libertà non esiste più.

———. 26 January 2007a. Berlusconi: Dopo di me c'è Fini.

———. 26 January 2007b. Maroni: Fini leader? Due dita negli occhi.

Cotta, M. and L. Verzichelli, 2003. The second Berlusconi government put to the test: A year of complications. In J. Blondel and P. Segatti, eds., *Italian Politics: the Second Berlusconi Government.* Oxford: Berghahn.

Cox, K. E., and L.J. Schoppa. 2002. Interaction effects in mixed-member electoral systems: theory and evidence from Germany, Japan, and Italy. *Comparative Political Studies* 35: 1027–53.

D'Alimonte, R., and S. Bartolini, eds. 2002. *Maggioritario finalmente? La transizione elettorale 1994–2001.* Bologna: Il Mulino.

D'Alimonte, R., and A. Chiaramonte. 1995. Il nuovo sistema elettorale Italiano: le opportunità e le scelte. In S. Bartolini, and R. D'Alimonte., eds., *Maggioritario ma non troppo.* Bologna: Il Mulino.

———. 2006. Proporzionale ma non solo. La riforma elettorale della Casa delle Libertà. *Il Mulino* 423: 34–45.

Dainotto, R. 2005. Review of John A. Agnew, *place and politics in modern Italy,* and P. Ginsborg, *Italy and its discontents. Journal of Modern History* 62: 460–62.

Della Vigna, S., and E. Kaplan. 2006. The Fox News effect: media bias and voting. Cambridge, MA: National Bureau of Economic Research. www.nber.org.papers/w12169

Diamanti, I. 1993. La Lega. *Geografia, storia e sociologia di un soggetto politico.* Rome: Donzelli Editrice.

———. 1994. Introduzione. In I. Diamanti and R. Mannheimer, eds. *Milano a Roma: Guida all'Italia elettorale di 1994.* Rome: Donzelli.

———. 1994. La Lega. In I. Diamanti and R. Mannheimer, eds. *Milano a Roma: Guida all'Italia elettorale di 1994.* Rome: Donzelli.

———. 1996. *Il male del Nord: Lega, localismo, secessione.* Rome: Donzelli.

———. 2003a. *Bianco, rosso, verde . . . e azzurro. Mappe e colori dell'Italia politica.* Bologna: Il Mulino.

———. 2003b. Il ritorno dello stato. L'Italia, dal regionalismo al neocentralismo. In P. Messina (ed.), *Sistemi locali e spazio europeo.* Rome: Carocci.

————. 2004. Tramonta il partito azzurro. Forza Italia non unisce più. *La Repubblica*. 29 June.

————. 2006a. Innocenti evasioni in un clima di complicità. *La Repubblica*. 1 October.

————. 2006b. Gli alleati inquieti nella Casa ostile. *La Repubblica,* 28 June.

————. 2006c. La destra senza radici si sbricola nelle città. *La Repubblica*. 31 May

————. 2007. The Italian centre-right and the centre-left: Between parties and "the Party." *West European Politics*, 30: 733–62.

Diamanti, I. and R. Mannheimer, R., eds. 1994. *Milano a Roma: Guida all'Italia elettorale del 1994*. Rome: Donzelli.

———— and E. Lello. 2005. The Casa della Libertà: A house of cards? *Modern Italy* 10: 9–35.

———— and Ceccarini, L. 2007. Catholics and politics after the Christian Democrats: the influential minority. *Journal of Modern Italian Studies*, 12: 37–59.

Di Virgilio, A. 1994. Dai partiti ai poli. La politica delle alleanze. *Rivista Italiana di Scienza Politica* 24, 493–547.

Dogan, M., and S. Rokkan, eds. 1969. *Quantitative Ecological Analysis in the Social Sciences.* Cambridge: MIT Press.

Dogan, M. 1967. Political cleavages and social stratification in France and Italy. In S. Lipset and S. Rokkan, eds., *Party systems and voter alignments*. New York: The Free Press.

Duara, P. 1995. *Rescuing history from the nation: Questioning narratives of modern China*. Chicago: University of Chicago Press.

Duverger, M. 1964. *Political parties: Their organization and activity in the modern state,* 3rd edition. London: Methuen.

Eagles, M., ed. 1995. *Spatial and contextual models in political research.* London: Taylor and Francis.

Elia, L. 2006. Il referendum costituzionale si avvicina. *Il Mulino* 424: 397–400.

Fabbrini, S. 2005. Il governo di partito in Italia: quali differenze tra Prima e Seconda Repubblica? *Italian Politics and Society* 60: 64–67.

Fargion, V., L. Morlino, and S. Profeti. 2006. Europeanisation and territorial representation in Italy. *West European Politics* 29: 757–783.

Feddersen, T. and W. Pesendorfer. 1999. Abstention in elections with asymmetric information and diverse preferences. *American Political Science Review* 93: 381–398.

Fella, S. 2004. Stuck in the middle? The role and positioning of the Alleanza Nazionale in the second Berlusconi government. Paper delivered to the Political Studies Association Annual Conference. Lincoln, England, 6–8 April.

Feltri, V. 2006. La verità sul patto Bossi-Silvio. Sapevano di perdere il referendum e hanno mentito. Pensando al futuro e alla rivincita. *Libero* (28 June), 1–2.

Ferrara, F. 2004. Electoral coordination and the strategic desertion of strong parties in compensatory mixed systems with negative vote transfers. *Electoral Studies* 23: 391–413.

Ferrera, M., and E. Gualmini. 2004. *Rescued by Europe? Social and labor market reforms in Italy from Maastricht to Berlusconi*. Amsterdam: Amsterdam University Press.

Follini, M. 2006. Teoria, prassi e ideologia del Berlusconismo. *Il Mulino* 424: 253–263.

Foot, J., 1996. The left opposition and the crisis: Rifondazione Comunista and La Rete. In S. Gundle and S. Parker, eds. The *New Italian Republic*. London: Routledge.

Foucault, M. 1980. *Power/knowledge: Selected interviews and other writings*. Brighton: Harvester.

Franchi, P. 2006. Le due italie divise e nemiche. *Corriere della Sera*, 11 April.

Frank, T. 2004. *What's the matter with Kansas: How conservatives won the heart of America*. New York: Metropolitan Books.

Galli della Loggia, E. 2006. Milano: la capitale della non politica, *Corriere della Sera*, 15 May.

Galli, G., and A. Prandi. 1970. *Patterns of political participation in Italy*. New Haven: Yale University Press.

Gangemi, G., and G. Riccamboni, eds. 1997. *Le elezioni della transizione*. Torino: UTET Libreria.

Ginsborg, P. 2003. *Italy and its discontents: Family, civil society, state, 1980–2001*. Basingstoke: Palgrave Macmillan.

———. 2004a. *Silvio Berlusconi: Television, power and patrimony*. London: Verso.

———. 2004b. *Il tempo di cambiare. Politica e potere della vita quotidiana*. Turin: Einaudi.

———. 2007. In the shadow of Berlusconi. *New York Review of Books*, 11 January: 50–52.

Girardin, S. 2006. Il senatur a Varese difende le piccole imprese. *La Padania*, 7 April: 1.

Goio, F., G. Maggioni, and M. Stoppino. 1983. *Il comportamento elettorale in Lombardia (1946–1980)*. Firenze: Le Monnier.

Golden, M. A. 2003. Electoral connections: The effects of the personal vote on political patronage, bureaucracy and legislation in postwar Italy. *British Journal of Political Science*, 33: 189–212.

———. 2004. International economic sources of regime change: How European integration undermined Italy's postwar party system. *Comparative Political Studies* 37: 1238–1274.

Goodin, R. E., and C. Tilly, eds. 2006. *The Oxford handbook of contextual political analysis.* Oxford: Oxford University Press.

Gould, P. 1970. Is statistix inferens the geographical name for a wild goose? *Economic Geography* 46, Supplement, Proceedings of the IGU Commission on Quantitative Methods: 439–448.

Griffith, D. 1987. *Spatial autocorrelation: A primer.* Washington, DC.: Association of American Geographers.

Griswold, W., and N. Wright. 2004. Cowbirds, locals, and the dynamic endurance of regionalism. *American Journal of Sociology* 109: 1411–1451.

Gschwend, T., R. J. Johnston, C. Pattie. 2003. Split-ticket patterns in mixed-member proportional elections systems: Estimates and analyses of their spatial variation at the German federal election, 1998. *British Journal of Political Science* 33: 109–127.

Guarnieri, C. 2006. *Il sistema politico italiano.* Bologna: Il Mulino.

Guerreri, P., and S. Iammarino. 2006. The rise of many Mezzogiorni: an empirical assessment of the internal differentiation of Italian southern regions. *European Urban and Regional Studies* 13: 167–178.

Gundle, S., and S. Parker, eds. 1996. *The new Italian republic: From the fall of the Berlin Wall to Berlusconi.* London: Routledge.

Hacking, I. 2004. Between Michel Foucault and Erving Goffman: Between discourse in the abstract and face-to-face interaction. *Economy and Society* 33: 277–302.

Haining, R. 2003. *Spatial data analysis: Theory and practice.* Cambridge: Cambridge University Press.

Hall, S. 1980. *Culture, media, language.* London: Hutchinson.

Hazen, R. 1996. Does center equal middle? Towards a conceptual delineation, with application to West European party systems. *Party Politics* 2: 209–228.

Hellman, S. 1992. The difficult birth of the Democratic Party of the Left. In S. Hellman and G. Pasquino, eds. *Italian Politics: a review, volume 7.* London: Pinter.

Hilder, P. 2005. Open parties? A map of 21st century democracy. *Open Democracy*, www.opendemocracy.net/articles/viewpopuparticle.jsp?id=3&articleid=2312.

Hopkin, J. 2005. Towards a chequebook democracy? Business, parties and the funding of politics in Italy and the United States. *Journal of Modern Italian Studies* 10: 43–58.

Huckfeldt, R., and J. Sprague. 1987. Networks in context: the social flow of political information. *American Political Science Review* 81: 1197–1216.

Ignazi, P. 1989. *Il polo escluso: Profilo sotrico del Movimento Sociale Italiano.* Bologna: Il Mulino.

———. 1992. *Dal Pci al Pds.* Bologna: Il Mulino.

Illy, R. 2006. Riccardo Illy: Più strade e meno tasse. Solo così Prodi può prendere il Nord. *Corriere della Sera*, 13 April.

ISPO 2006. I giovani decisive per l'Unione, Polo rilanciato dall'effetto tasse. Istituto Cattaneo 2006. Elezioni Politiche 2006. www.cattaneo.org.

ITANES 2001. *Perché ha vinto il centro-destra?* Bologna: Il Mulino.

Jampaglia, C. 2006. Stefano Draghi: Sono tornati a votare i delusi della CDL. *Liberazione*, 14 April.

Janda, K. 1980. *Political parties: A cross-national survey.* New York: The Free Press.

Johnston, R. J., 1986. The neighborhood effect revisited: Spatial science or political regionalism? *Environment and Planning D* 4: 41–55.

———. 1992. *A question of place.* Oxford: Blackwell.

Johnston, R. J., and C. Pattie. 1992. Class dealignment and the regional polarization of voting patterns in Great Britain, 1964–1987. *Political Geography* 11: 73–86.

———. 1999. Constituency campaign intensity and split-ticket voting: New Zealand's first election under MMP, 1996. *Political Science* 51: 164–181.

———. 2000. Ecological inference and entropy maximizing: An alternative procedure for split-ticket voting. *Political Analysis* 8: 333–345.

Katz, R., and P. Ignazi, eds. 1996. *Italian politics: The year of the tycoon.* Boulder: Westview Press.

Katz, R. 1973. The attribution of variance in electoral returns: An alternative measurement technique. *American Political Science Review* 67: 817–828.

Katz, R., and P. Mair, eds. 1994. *How parties organize: Change and adaptation in party organizations in Western democracies.* London: Sage.

Katz, E., and P. F. Lazarsfeld. 1955. *Personal influence: The part played by people in the flow of mass communications.* New York: Free Press.

Kertzer, D. 1996. *Politics and symbols: the Italian Communist Party and the fall of Communism.* New Haven: Yale University Press.

Key, V. O. 1955. A theory of critical elections. *The Journal of Politics* 17 (1), 3–18.

Kim, J., E. Elliot., D. M. Wang. 2003. A spatial analysis of county-level outcomes in US presidential elections: 1988–2000. *Electoral Studies* 22: 741–761.

Kinder, D. R. 2006. Politics and the life cycle. *Science* 312 (30 June): 1905–1908.

King, G. 1996. Why context should not count. *Political Geography* 15: 159–164.

———. 1997. *A solution to the ecological inference problem.* Princeton: Princeton University Press.

———. 2002. *EI: A Program for Ecological Inference v. 2.65.* Cambridge, MA: Harvard University.

Kitschelt, H. 1992. The formation of party systems in East Central Europe. *Politics & Society* 20: 7–50.

————. 1995. Formation of party cleavages in post-Communist democracies. *Party Politics* 1: 143–160.

Lazar, M. 2007. *Democrazia all prova. L'Italia dopo Berlusconi.* Rome/Bari: Laterza.

Legnante, G. 2004. The 2003 local elections: First local and then national defeats for the Cosa delle Libertà. In S. Fabbrini and V. Della Sala, eds., *Italy between Europeanization and Domestic Politics.* Oxford: Berghahn.

Leonardi, R. 2003. The denationalization of Italian politics and policy making. In R. Leonardi and M. Fedele, eds. *Italy: Politics and policy.* Volume 2. Aldershot: Ashgate.

Lipman-Blumen, J. 2006. *The allure of toxic leaders.* New York: Oxford University Press.

Livolsi, M., and U. Volli, eds. 1995. *La communicazione politica tra prima e seconda repubblica.* Milan: Franco Angeli.

Lumley, R., and J. Morris, eds. 1997. *The new history of the Italian South: The Mezzogiorno revisited.* Exeter: University of Exeter Press.

Magnier, A. 2004. Between institutional learning and re-legitimization: Italian mayors in the unending reform. *International Journal of Urban and Regional Research* 28: 166–182.

Mair, P. 2006. Ruling the void: the hollowing of Western democracy. *New Left Review* 42: 25–51.

Mannheimer, R. 1994. Forza Italia. In I. Diamanti and R. Mannheimer, eds. *Milano a Roma: Guida all'Italia elettorale di 1994.* Rome: Donzetti.

————. 2002. Le elezioni del 2001 e la mobilitazione drammatizante. In G. Pasquino, ed. *Dall'Ulivo al governo Berlusconi. Le elezioni del 13 maggio e il sistema politico italiano.* Bologna: Il Mulino.

————. 2004. I flussi elettorali. *Corriere della Sera,* 20 June.

————. 2006a. Indeciso un terzo degli elettori. *Corriere della Sera,* 14 March.

————. 2006b. La manovra delude gli elettori dell'Unione. *Corriere della Sera,* 10 October.

————. 2006c. Unipol, l'Unione cala ma resta in vantaggio. *Corriere della Sera,* 18 January.

————. 2006d. Cdl, continua la rimonta, FI in crescita. *Corriere della Sera,* 21 February.

Mannheimer, R., and G. Sani. 2001. *La conquista degli astenuti.* Bologna: Il Mulino.

Massey, D. 1999. *Power-geometries and the politics of space-time.* Heidelberg: University of Heidelberg, Institute of Geography.

Mastropaolo, A. 2000. *Antipolitica.* Naples: L'Ancora.

McAllister, I. 1987. Social context, turnout and the vote: Australian and British comparisons. *Political Geography Quarterly* 6: 17–30.

McCarthy, P. 1996. Forza Italia: The overwhelming success and consequent problems of a virtual party In R. Katz and P. Ignazi, eds. *Italian politics: The year of the tycoon.* Boulder: Westview Press.

————. 1997. *The crisis of the Italian state.* London: Macmillan.

Messina, P. 1997. Persistenza e mutamento nelle subculture politiche territoriali. In G. Gangemi and G. Riccamboni, eds. *Le elezioni della transizione. Il sistema politicop italiano alla prova del voto 1994–1996.* Turin: UTET.

————., ed. 2001. *Regolazione politica dello sviluppo locale. Veneto ed Emilia Romagna a confronto.* Turin: UTET.

Messina, S. 2006. Dalla "porcata" all'autogol e Calderoli lanciò l'Unione. *La Repubblica*, 12 April.

Morlino, L. 1996. Crisis of parties and change of party system in Italy. *Party Politics* 2: 5–30.

Nardulli, P. 1995. The concept of a critical realignment, electoral behavior, and political change. *American Political Science Review* 89: 10–22.

Natale, P. 2006. Tradimenti e conferme come è cambiato il consenso degli Italiani rispetto alle politiche del 2001. *La Stampa*, 12 April.

Nelken, D. 1996. A legal revolution? The judges and Tangentopoli. In S. Gundle and S. Parker, eds. *The New Italian Republic.* London: Routledge.

Newell, J. 2006. The Italian election of May 2006: Myths and realities. *West European Politics* 29: 802–813.

Novelli, E. 1995. *Dalla tv di partito al partito della tv. Televisione e politica in Italia.* Florence: La Nuova Italia.

O'Loughlin, J. V., C. Flint, and L. Anselin. 1994. The geography of the Nazi vote: Context, confession and class in the Reichstag election of 1930. *Annals of the Association of American Geographers* 84: 351–380.

————, M. E. Shin, and P. Talbot. 1996. Political geographies and political cleavages in the Russian parliamentary elections of 1993 and 1995. *Post-Soviet Geography and Economics* 37: 355–386.

O'Sullivan, D., and D. Unwin. 2003. *Geographic information analysis.* Hoboken: John Wiley and Sons.

Ostellino, P. 2006. L'inflazione delle promesse, *Corriere della Sera*, 5 April.

Paba, G., and R. Paloscia. 1994. Dal Bel Paese alla città diffusa. In P. Ginsborg, ed. *Stato dell'Italia.* Milan: Il Saggiatore.

Pagnoncelli, N. 2001. *Opinioni in percentuale. I sondaggi tra politica e informazione.* Rome-Bari: Laterza.

Pajetta, G. 1994. *Il grande camaleonte. Episodi passioni, avventure del leghismo.* Milan: Feltrinelli.

Panebianco, A. 1988. *Political parties: Organization and power.* Cambridge: Cambridge University Press.

————. 2006. Il nord lontano dai vincitori. *Corriere della Sera,* 13 April.

Pappalardo, A. 1995. La nuova legge elettorale in parlamento: chi, come e perchè. In S. Bartolini and R. D'Alimonte, eds. *Maggioritario ma non troppo.* Bologna: Il Mulino.

————. 2002. Il sistema italiano fra bipolarismo e destrutturazione. In G. Pasquino, ed. *Dall'Ulivo al governo Berlusconi. Le elezioni del 13 maggio 2001 e il sistema politico italiano.* Bologna: Il Mulino.

————. 2006. Italian bipolarism and the elections of 2006. End of the line or just a connecting stop? *Journal of Modern Italian Studies.* 11: 472–493.

Parker, S. 2006. Managing the political field: Italian regions and the territorialisation of politics in the Second Republic. *Journal of Southern Europe and the Balkans* 8: 235–253.

————. 2007. Introduction: A tale of two Italies—Continuities and change in the Italian republic, 1994–2006. *Modern Italy* 12: 1–15.

Parker, S., and P. Natale. 2002. Parliamentary elections in Italy, May 2002. *Electoral Studies* 21: 665–73 [2003. Erratum: Parliamentary elections in Italy, May 2001. *Electoral Studies,* 22: 763]

Pasquino, G. 1985. *Restituire lo scettro al principe. Proposte di riforma istituzionale.* Rome: Laterza.

————. 2002. *Il sistema politico italiano. Autorità, istituzioni, società.* Bologna: Bononia University Press.

————. 2003. The government, the opposition and the President of the Republic under Berlusconi. *Journal of Modern Italian Studies,* 8: 485–500.

————. 2005. Berlusconismo senza Berlusconi? *La Rivista dei Libri,* September. www.larivistadeilibri.it/2005/09/pasquino.html

————. 2007. The five faces of Silvio Berlusconi: The knight of antipolitics. *Modern Italy* 12: 39–54.

Pattie, C., and R. J. Johnston. 1997. Local economic contexts and changing party allegiances at the 1992 British general election. *Party Politics* 3: 79–96.

————. 2003. Local battles in a national landslide: constituency campaigning at the 2001 British general election. *Political Geography* 22: 381–414.

Perna, T. 2006. *Destra e sinistra nell'Europa del XXI secolo.* Milan: Altreconomia.

Petrusewicz, M. 2004. Review of *Place and Politics in Modern Italy. Journal of Interdisciplinary History,* 35: 303–306.

Piattoni, S. 1999. Politica locale e sviluppo economico nel Mezzogiorno. *Stato e Mercato:* 55: 117–149.

————. 2005a. *Il clientelismo. L'Italia in prospettiva comparata.* Rome: Carocci.

————. 2005b. Review of I. Diamanti, *Bianco, rosso, verde . . . e azzurro. Rivista Italiana di Scienza Politica* 35: 165–167.

Poli, E. 2001. *Forza Italia. Strutture, leadership e radicamento territoriale.* Bologna: Il Mulino.

Przeworski, A. 1991. *Democracy and the market: Political and economic reforms in Eastern Europe and Latin America.* New York: Cambridge University Press.

Putnam, R. D., with R. Leonardi, and R. Nanetti. 1993. *Making democracy work: Civic traditions in modern Italy.* Princeton: Princeton University Press.

Ramella, F. 2005. *Cuore rosso? Viaggio politico nell'Italia di mezzo.* Rome: Donzelli.

Rampulla, F. C. 1997. La legge Bassanini e le autonomie locali. *Il Politico* 62: 131–142.

Reed, S. R. 2001. Duverger's law is working in Italy. *Comparative Political Studies* 34: 313–27.

La Repubblica. 2006. Berlusconi come lo storico nazista. Bufera sulla frase di Buttiglione. September 14.

———. 2006. UDC, Follini si prepara all'addio tra rimpianti dei big del partito. October 10.

———. 2006. Cdl, l'allarme di Maroni: Minata la leadership di Berlusconi. October 23.

Riccamboni, G. 1994. L'area bianca. In I. Diamanti and R. Mannheimer, eds. *Milano a Roma: Guida all'Italia elettorale di 1994.* Rome: Donzelli.

———. 1997. Ritorno al futuro? La transizione nell'ex subcultura bianca, in Gangemi, G., G. Riccamboni, eds., *Le elezioni della transizione. Il sistema politico italiano alla prova del voto 1994–1996.* Torino: UTET.

Ricolfi, L. 1994. Il voto proporzionale e il nuovo spazio politico italiano. *Rivista Italiana di Scienza Politica* 24: 587–629.

———. 2005. *Dossier Italia: A che punto è il Contratto con gli italiani?* Bologna: Il Mulino.

———. 2006. *Tempo scaduto. Il Contratto con gli italiani alla prova dei fatti.* Bologna: Il Mulino.

Riotta, G. 2006. Berlusconi, come Bush, premiato da chi detesta la politica. *Corriere della Sera,* 11 April.

Rodriguez, M. 1994. La communicazione politica. In I. Diamanti and R. Mannheimer, eds. *Milano a Roma. Guida all'Italia elettorale del 1994.* Rome: Donzelli.

Romano, S. 1993. *L'Italia scappata di mano.* Milan: Longanesi.

———. 2007. La politica del teatrino. Le strategie indecifrabili del Cavaliere. *Corriere della Sera,* 1 February.

Sabetti, F. 2000. *The search for good government: Understanding the paradox of Italian democracy.* Montreal: McGill-Queen's University Press.

Salvadori, M.L. 1994. *Storia d'Italia e crisi di regime. Alle radici della politica italiana.* Bologna: Il Mulino.

Salvati, M. 2003. Behind the cold war: rethinking the left, the state and civil society in Italy (1940s–1970s). *Journal of Modern Italian Studies* 8: 556–577.

Sani, G. 1994. Una vigilia di incertezze. *Rivista Italiana di Scienza Politica* 24: 403–25.

Sapelli, G. 1994. *Cleptocrazia. Il meccanismo unico della corruzione tra economia e politica.* Milan: Feltrinelli.

————. 1997. The transformation of the Italian party system. *Journal of Modern Italian Studies* 2: 167–187.

Saraceno, P. 1988. *L'unificazione economico italiano è ancora lontana.* Bologna: Il Mulino.

Sartori, G. 1989. Videopolitica. *Rivista Italiana di Scienza Politica* 19: 185–198.

————. 2006a. Il bipolarismo frainteso. Il nostro è ancora un sistema parlamentare. *Corriere della Sera,* 20 April.

————. 2006b. Il "porcellum" da eliminare. *Corriere della Sera,* 1 November.

————. 2007. Con il Tatarellum di male in peggio. Le ipotesi sulla riforma del sistema elettorale. *Corriere della Sera,* 9 February.

Sbisà, M. 1996. Politica e racconta: il caso delle elezioni italiane del 1994. *Polis* 10: 197–217.

Schlesinger, P. 1990. The Berlusconi phenomenon. In Z.G. Baranski and R. Lumley, eds. *Culture and conflict in postwar Italy.* London: St. Martin's Press.

Sciolla, L. 2004. *La sfida dei valori. Rispetto delle regole e rispetto dei diretti in Italia.* Bologna: Il Mulino.

Segatti, P. 1994. I programmi elettorali e il ruolo dei mass media. *Rivista Italiana di Scienza Politica* 24: 465–491.

Shin, M. E. 2001. The politicization of place in Italy. *Political Geography* 20: 331–352.

Shin, M.E., and J. Agnew. 2002. The geography of party replacement in Italy, 1987–1996. *Political Geography* 21: 221–242.

Shin, M., J. Agnew, S. Breau, and P. Richardson. 2006. Place and the geography of Italian export performance. *European Urban and Regional Studies* 13: 195–208.

Solt, F. 2004. Civics or structure? Revisiting the origins of democratic quality in the Italian regions. *British Journal of Political Science* 34: 123–135.

Sottocornola, F. 2006. Inchiesta perché i signori della statistica hanno sbagliato le previsioni. *Il Mondo.* 15 April.

Stella, G.A. 2005. *Tribù S.P.A. Foto di gruppo con cavaliere bis.* Milan: Feltrinelli.

Stille, A. 2006. *The sack of Rome.* London: Penguin.

Street, J. 2004. Celebrity politicians: popular culture and political representation. *British Journal of Politics and International Relations* 6: 435–452.

Taddia, M. 2004. Italy's broadcast news. Silvio Berlusconi's media empire is extending to radio. *Financial Times,* 19 October: 11.

Tarchi, M., 1997. *Dal Msi ad An.* Bologna: Il Mulino.

————. 2003. *L'Italia populista*. Bologna: Il Mulino.

Taylor, M. 2006. *Rationality and the ideology of disconnection*. Cambridge: Cambridge University Press.

Thompson, J.B. 2000. *Political scandal: Power and visibility in the media age*. Cambridge: Polity Press.

Tobler, W. 1963. Geographic ordering of information. *Canadian Geographer* 11: 203–5.

Travaglio, M. 1995. *Il Pollaio delle Libertà. Detti, disdetti e contraddetti*. Firenze: Vallecchi.

Trigilia, C., 1986. *Grandi partiti e piccole imprese*. Bologna: Il Mulino.

Turano, G. 2006. *Calciogate*. Milan: Il Saggiatore.

Valussi, G., ed. 1987. *L'Italia geoeconomica*. Turin: UTET.

Vandelli, L. 2002. *Devolution e altre storie. Paradossi, ambiguità e rischi di un progetto politico*. Bologna: Il Mulino.

VareseNews. 2006. La Lega Nord ha illuso e poi venduto il popolo padano, 5 November http://www3.varesenews.it/varese/articolo.php?id=59264

Ventrone, A. 2005. *Il nemico interno. Immagini e simboli della lotta politica nell'Italia del '900*. Rome: Donzelli.

Venturino, F., ed. 2005. *Elezioni e personalizzazione della politica*. Rome: ARACNE.

Vignati, R. 2006. La sfiducia degli italiani nella classe politica. *Il Mulino* 423: 146–150.

Wellhofer, E. S. 2001. Party realignment and voter transition in Italy, 1987–1996. *Comparative Political Studies* 34: 156–186.

Wise, P. 2005. Southern Europe's airwave: Higher television viewerships and lower costs are spurring on growth. *Financial Times*, 19 April: 13.

Zinn, D. L. 2001. *La raccommandazione. Clientelismo vecchio e nuovo*. Rome: Donzelli.

————. 2007. I Quindici Giorni di Scanzano: Identity and social protest in the new South. *Journal of Modern Italian Studies*, 12: 189–206.

Zolo, D. 1999. From "historic compromise" to "telecratic compromise": notes for a history of political communication between the first and second republics. *Media, Culture & Society* 21: 727–741.

Zuckerman, A.S., ed. 2005. *The social logic of politics: Personal networks as contexts for political behavior*. Philadelphia: Temple University Press.

Index

Michael Shin is Associate Professor at the University of California, Los Angeles. His publications include articles on Italian politics and society, political geography and globalization.

John Agnew is Professor of Geography at the University of California, Los Angeles. He is author or co-author of *Hegemony: The New Shape of Global Power* (Temple), *Place and Politics, The United States in the World Economy, The Geography of the World Economy, Geopolitics*, and *Place and Politics in Modern Italy*, among other titles, as well as co-editor of *American Space/Amercian Place*.